Orange Line 1

Workbook

Herausgeber: Dr. Frank Haß

Ernst Klett Verlag
Stuttgart • Leipzig

Go on a tour around your book!

Hier könnt ihr ein Spiel spielen, das euch dabei hilft, euer Schulbuch besser kennen zu lernen. Dazu arbeitet ihr in Dreier-Gruppen zusammen und versucht, so schnell wie möglich alle Fragen zu beantworten. Die Lösungen sind im Schulbuch versteckt. Kreist die richtigen Lösungen ein. Wenn ihr fertig seid, sucht euch eine andere Gruppe, die auch fertig ist, und vergleicht eure Lösungen. Wer hat die meisten richtigen Antworten?

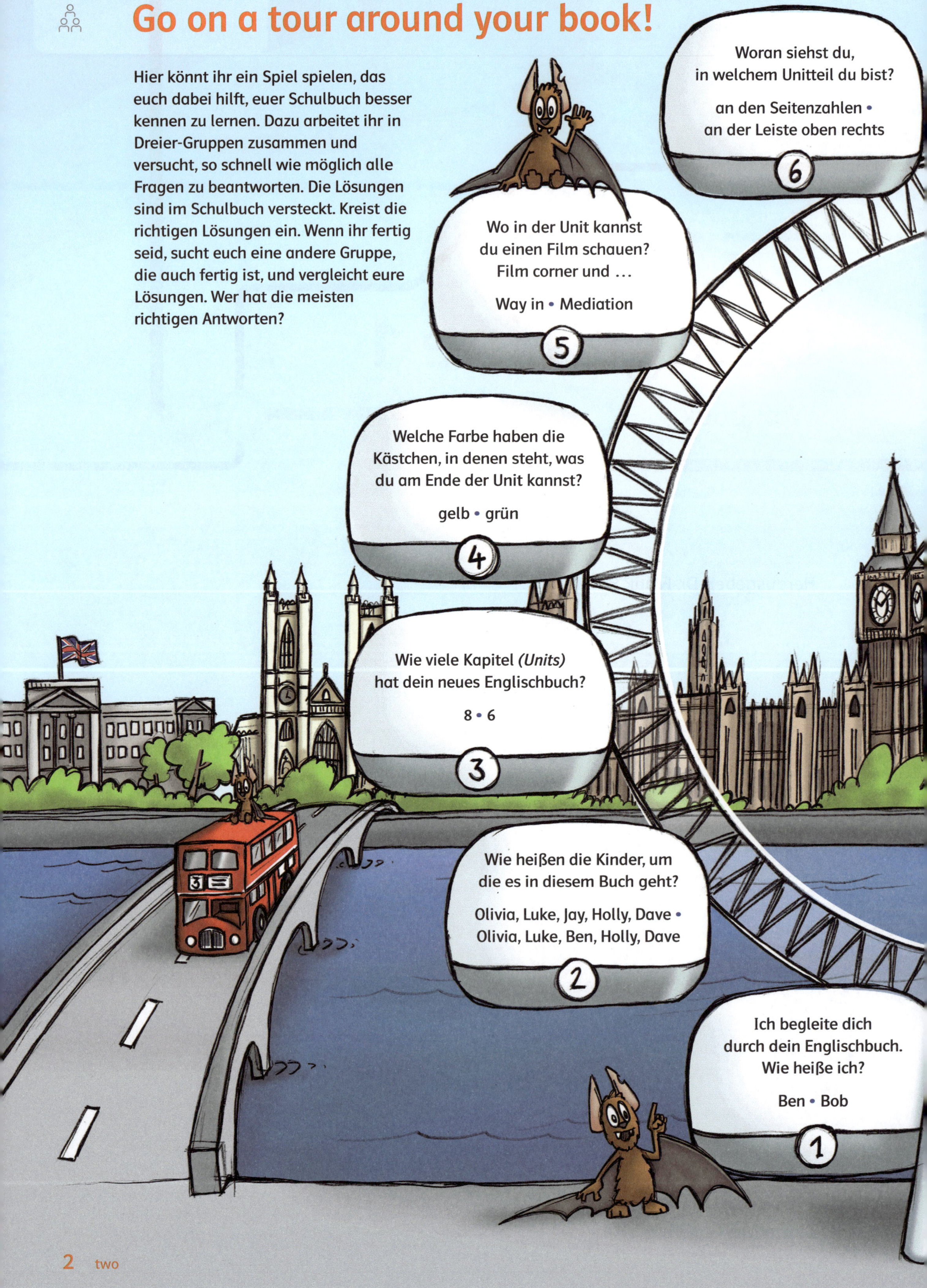

Das London Eye ist ein großes Riesenrad und steht an der Themse. Von dort hast du einen tollen Überblick über London. Genauso gewinnst du mit diesem Spiel einen Überblick über dein Schulbuch.

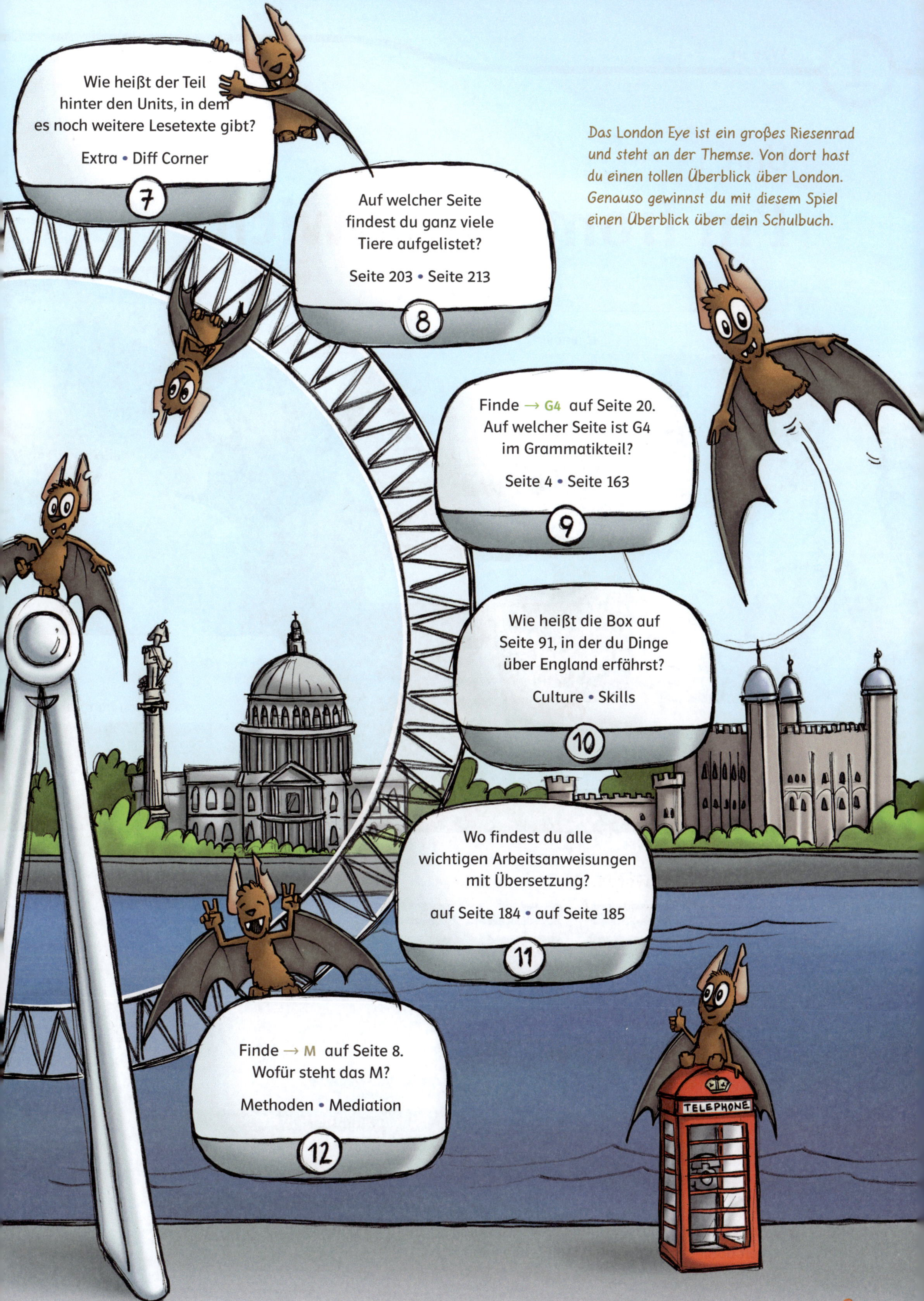

7
Wie heißt der Teil hinter den Units, in dem es noch weitere Lesetexte gibt?

Extra • Diff Corner

8
Auf welcher Seite findest du ganz viele Tiere aufgelistet?

Seite 203 • Seite 213

9
Finde → G4 auf Seite 20. Auf welcher Seite ist G4 im Grammatikteil?

Seite 4 • Seite 163

10
Wie heißt die Box auf Seite 91, in der du Dinge über England erfährst?

Culture • Skills

11
Wo findest du alle wichtigen Arbeitsanweisungen mit Übersetzung?

auf Seite 184 • auf Seite 185

12
Finde → M auf Seite 8. Wofür steht das M?

Methoden • Mediation

Unit 1

I'm from Greenwich

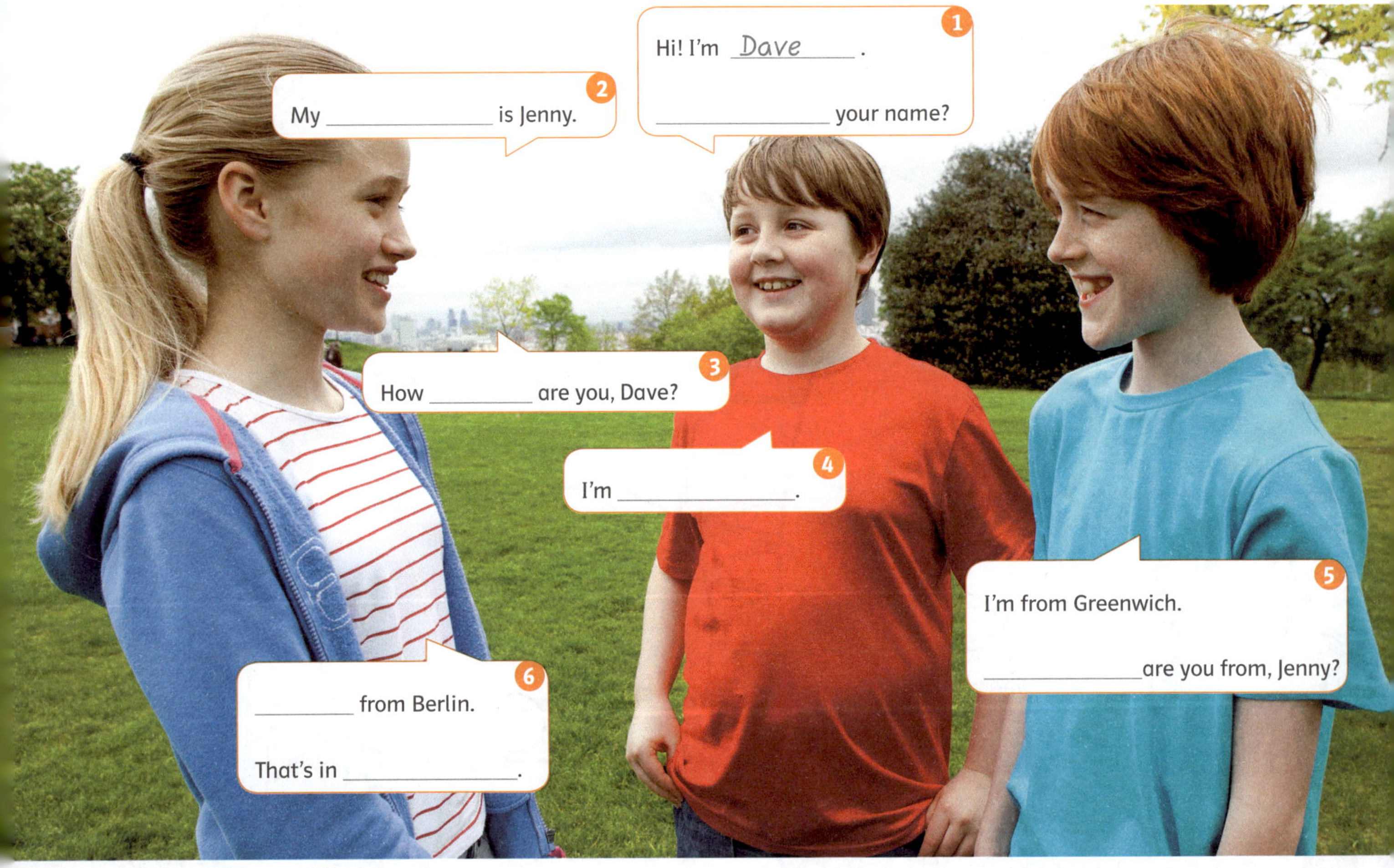

12/2

1 Put in the right words.

Where · Dave ✓ · What's · name · I'm · Germany · old · twelve

13/3

2 What's your name?

a) Verbinde die Fragen und Antworten.

Hi!	I'm twelve.
What's your name?	I'm from Berlin. That's in Germany.
How old are you?	My name is Jenny.
Where are you from, Jenny?	Hello.

b) Bewege dich im Klassenzimmer. Suche dir eine Partnerin / einen Partner. Spielt dann gemeinsam den Dialog aus a) nach.

1
15/4

1 (SOUNDS) Listen and tick ✓ the words with [ð].

☐ 

☐ 

☐ 

☐ 

15/5

2 (WRITING) Find the family words.

a)

dadbrothersistermothermumfather

1. dad
2. ______
3. ______
4. ______
5. ______
6. ______

b)

grandfatheruncleparentsauntgrandmothercousin

1. ______
2. ______
3. ______
4. ______
5. ______
6. ______

15/6

3 A quiz

a) Welches Wort passt nicht?

1.	2.	3.	4.
a) mother	a) cat	a) crazy	a) twelve
b) dog	b) guinea pig	b) cool	b) football
c) father	c) bike	c) nice	c) seven
d) sister	d) dog	d) brother	d) three

b) Denke dir für deine Partnerin / deinen Partner ein Quiz wie in a) aus.

1. a) ______
   b) ______
   c) ______
   d) ______

2. a) ______
   b) ______
   c) ______
   d) ______

16/9

4 Match the words.

my family and I	it
Mum and Dad	he
bike	she
Claire	we
my Dad	they

16/10

5 Look at Claire's family photos.

a) Choose the right word.

1. Desmond and Lucy are / is in the garden.
2. I am / are with Lucy.
3. Janet are / is Olivia's mum.
4. Desmond am / is in the garden.
5. Olivia and her mum is / are in the park.
6. I am / is a Fraser family fan.

b) Put in am, is or are.

This ________ a nice photo of the Fraser family. I ________ next to Desmond. He ________ cool. Olivia ________ eleven and Lucy is five. Here we ________ crazy.

17/11

6 Complete the chart.

long form	short form
I am	I'm
you are	
	he's
she is	
	it's
we are	
	they're

17/12

7 Put in short forms.

I'm ✓ | they're (2x) | we're | he's

Hello, it's Sid. Yes, I'm ______ Dave's cat.

Dave? ______ twelve. Yes, ______ friends.

Dave and his family? ______ from Greenwich.

Dogs? ______ crazy!

17/13

8 (READING) Find the names for the family tree.

a) 1. Karen and Bill are Nancy's mother and father.
2. Harry is Nancy's brother.

b) 1. Margaret and Derek are Nancy's aunt and uncle.
2. Nancy and Harry are Michael's cousins.

1 (SOUNDS) Listen, write and say.

2 17/13

this	brother ✓	they	the
with	that	mother	father

Hilfreiche Tipps zur Lautschrift findest du in deinem Buch auf Seite 183.

1. [ˈbrʌðə] brother
2. [ˈmʌðə] ____________
3. [ðɪs] ____________
4. [ðeɪ] ____________
5. [wɪð] ____________
6. [ˈfɑːðə] ____________
7. [ðə] ____________
8. [ðæt] ____________

2 (SPEAKING) Make a dialogue.

17/13

a) Complete the dialogue.

Partner A	Partner B
Hi! What's your name?	
	Hello! My name is ____________. What's ____________?
My name is ____________.	
	How old are you?
I'm ____________. And you?	
	I'm ____________.
I'm from ____________. Where are you ____________?	
	I'm from ____________.
My mother is from ____________. And your mother?	
	My mother is from ____________, my father is from ____________.
Bye.	
	Bye.

b) Act the dialogue with a partner.

1 (LISTENING) Listen to the words and put a circle ◯ in the picture.

18/2 3

2 Look at the room and put in on, in, under, next to.

19/5

1. The football is under ______ the bed.
2. The chair is ______ the table.
3. The books are ______ the shelf.
4. The boxes are ______ the table.
5. The mobile is ______ the box.
6. The T-shirts are ______ the chair.

3 Put in There is or There are and the right word from exercise 1.

19/6

1. There is ______ one green football ______ under the bed.
2. There are ______ three ______ on the chair.
3. ______ one white ______ on the table.
4. ______ one blue ______ next to the brown table.
5. ______ eight ______ on the shelf.

20/10

4 Complete the questions and answers.

a) Put in Is or Are.

1. Are ______ you from Germany?
2. ______ your friend a football fan?
3. ______ your mobile black?
4. ______ you a cat fan?

b) Ask your partner and write the answers.

– Yes, I am. / No, I'm from … .
– ______
– ______
– ______

20/10

5 (WRITING) Draw the things in the room.

a) Draw a football, four books, a computer, two guinea pigs and a T-shirt in your room.

Your room

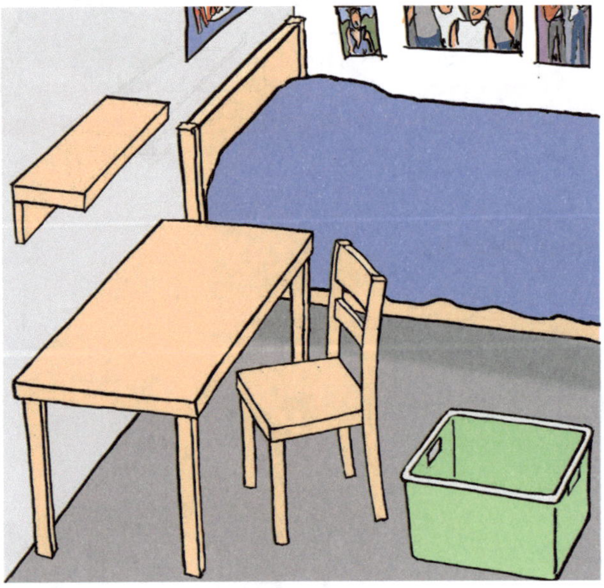

Your partner's room

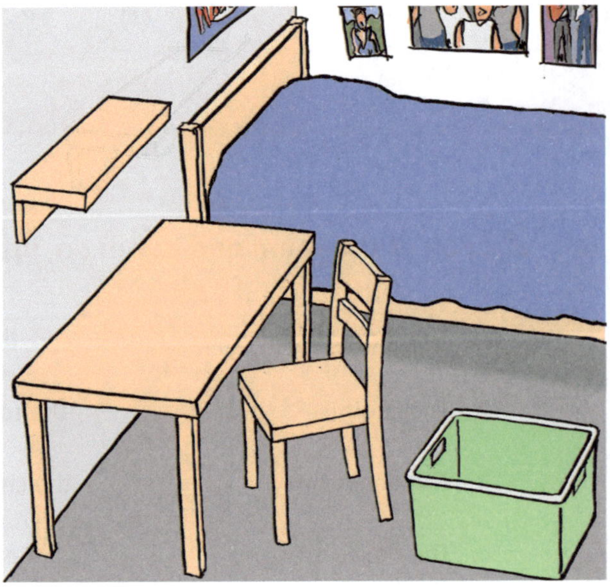

b) Write four questions about your partner's room with Is or Are.

1. computer • on the shelf — Is the computer on the shelf?
2. guinea pigs • in the box — Are ______
3. T-shirt • on the bed — ______
4. books • on the table — ______
5. football • under the bed — ______

c) Ask your partner the questions from b). Listen to his / her answers and draw the things in his / her room.

Example: Is the computer on the shelf? – No, it's on the table.

6 Put in Who, What or Where.

20/11

1. What ____________ is it? – It's a T-shirt.

2. ____________ is Ben? – He's in the box.

3. ____________ is he? – He's Luke.

4. ____________ is it? – It's a ball.

7 Make questions.

21/12

a) Put in What, Who, Where, Are or Is.

1. What ____________ 's your name? – My name is Zarina.
2. ____________ are you from? – I'm from Greenwich.
3. ____________ is next to you? – It's my brother Kiran.
4. ____________ he five? – No, he's four.
5. ____________ your mum and dad from England? – Yes, they're from England.

b) Act the dialogue with a partner.

8 (LISTENING) A poem

21/14

4

a) Hör dir das Gedicht an und lies es zusammen mit deiner Partnerin / deinem Partner laut vor.

Who is for friends and family too.
Who is a cool friend? – Luke, it's you!

Where is for under and next to and there.
Where is my T-shirt? – It's on the chair.

What is for rooms and books white and red.
What's in your room? – My chair and my bed.

b) Mache dein eigenes Gedicht, indem du die unterstrichenen Wörter durch eigene ersetzt.

1 (READING) Right or wrong? Tick ✓ the right box.

22/2

	right	wrong
1. Lucy is in the garden.	✓	☐
2. Olivia and her dad are in the house.	☐	☐
3. There's a ladder in the garden.	☐	☐
4. The tree house is cool.	☐	☐
5. Claire is on the ladder.	☐	☐
6. Olivia is in the tree house.	☐	☐
7. In the night Holly is in the tree house with Olivia.	☐	☐

2 (READING) Finish the words.

22/2

1. Claire is in the h... .
2. Olivia's dad is in the t... .
3. There's wood and there's a l... .
4. Olivia and her dad are b... .
5. The plan for the tree house is g... !
6. Holly and Olivia san s... in the tree house.
7. In the n... Olivia and Holly are in the tree house.
8. There's a funny n... .
9. Holly is in a sweet d... .

The story is about Olivia's ☐☐☐☐ ☐☐☐☐☐ .

3 (WRITING) What's your story?

23/5

Denke dir ein anderes Ende für die Geschichte aus. Fertige dazu eine Zeichnung an und schreibe dazu einen passenden Satz.

____

____

____

____

1 What's the name of the room?

25/2

k ______ b ______ b ______ l ______

2 (VIEWING) Who is in the rooms?

25/2

a) Watch the film again. Colour the right circle ◯.

b) Stelle pantomimisch dar, in welchem Zimmer aus dem Film du dich befindest.
Deine Partnerin / dein Partner versucht zu erraten, um welches Zimmer es sich handelt.
Wechselt euch ab.

1 Checkpoint

1. Löse alle Aufgaben.
2. Überprüfe deine Lösungen online. Gib dazu den 🌐 -Code (nach Ziel 5) auf www.klett.de ein.
3. Gib dir selbst Punkte. Wenn du weniger als die Hälfte der Punkte hast, male das Kästchen rot aus und übe auf den Step by step-Seiten (z. B. bei Unit 1 auf S. 16 – 17).

Ziel 1: Ich kann mich selbst vorstellen.

→ ◎ 6m2t9e

Look at Linda's poster. What can she say?

Hi! My name is Linda ______ . ______ Steve's sister.

I'm ______ London. That's in ______ .

I'm a ______ fan. Football is ______ .

My ______ is seven.

6P

→ p. 16/1

Ziel 2: Ich kann über meine Familie sprechen.

→ ◎ cv7n5x

brothers | sister | family ✓ | mum and dad | pets

"This is my family ______ .

Kate and Rob are my ______ .

Max and Steve are my ______ .

Fay is my ______ . The ______

are here too. Two cats and one dog."

4P

→ p. 16/2

Ziel 3: Ich kann mich über mein Zimmer unterhalten.

→ ◎ vk4u84 → ◎ 78jw3k

This is Harry's bedroom. Look at the picture and write the answers.

1. Are there books? Yes, there are three books. ______
2. Where are they? They're ______
3. Is there a box? Yes, there is ______
4. Is it under the chair? No, it's ______
5. What's on the bed? There ______

4P

→ p. 16/3

Ziel 4: Ich kann eine Bildergeschichte verstehen.

→ de57k9

a) Put the pictures in the right order. Write the number in the box.

b) Match the sentences with the pictures.

☐ Luke: Sherlock! Thanks.

☐ Luke's bedroom is a mess.

☐ It's ready! Now Luke's bedroom is nice.

☐ Luke: Oh, Sherlock. My room is a mess!

8P

→ p. 17/4

Ziel 5: Ich kann zwei Personen miteinander bekannt machen.

a) Jana möchte Steve kennenlernen. Stell ihn vor.

Das ist *Steve.* ______

Er kommt aus ______

Er fragt: Woher ______

Er hat ______

Er möchte wissen: Hast ______

b) Nun stelle Jana auf Englisch vor.

This is ______

She is from ______

She has ______

Jana is a ______

And you?

8P

→ p. 17/5

Lösungen online
2f55hf

Ziel 1: Ich kann mich vorstellen.

○ a) Welche Sätze brauchst du, um dich vorzustellen? Kreise sie ein.

The ... is under the bed.	Hello! My name is ... ✓	... the football?	I'm ... years old.
I'm from ...	The ... is brown.	That's in ...	I'm a ... fan.

○ b) Schreibe die eingekreisten Sätze auf und fülle die Lücken mit Informationen über dich aus.

Hello! My name is ______________________

____

____

○ Ziel 2: Ich kann über meine Familie sprechen.

Was erzählt Lucy über ihre Familie? Fülle die Lücken aus.

1. Hello, my name is Lucy.
   I'm five and this is my *family*.
2. Here's Olivia. She's my ____________.
3. I have no ____________.
4. This is Desmond. He's our ____________.
5. Claire is my ____________. She's nice.

Wenn du über deine eigene Familie sprechen willst, kannst du Lucys Sätze als Muster nehmen.

○ Ziel 3: Ich kann mich über mein Zimmer unterhalten.

Wo ist Ben? Schreibe die Vorgaben auf die richtige Linie.

- under the table
- next to the table
- on the table
- in the box

____

____

____

____

Ziel 4: Ich kann eine Bildergeschichte verstehen.

○ **a)** Auf welchen Bildern kommt Sherlock vor? Sieh dir an, was Sherlock auf den Bildern macht und entscheide, welcher Satz zu welchem Bild passt. Die blau unterstrichenen Wörter können dir helfen.

Oh, Sherlock. Bild: ________

Sherlock. Thanks! Bild: ________

○ **b)** Sieh dir nun die blau unterstrichenen Wörter an und überlege, welcher Satz zu den übrig gebliebenen Bildern passt.

It's ready. Luke's bedroom is nice. Bild: ________

Luke's bedroom is a mess. Bild: ________

○ **c)** Bringe nun die Bilder in die richtige Reihenfolge.

1. ________ 2. ________ 3. ________ 4. ________

Ziel 5: Ich kann zwei Personen miteinander bekannt machen.

○

Welche Sätze gehören zusammen? Verbinde sie.

1. Hello! My name is Steve.
2. I'm from Liverpool.
3. Where are you from?
4. I have one brother.
5. Do you have brothers or sisters?

a) Er kommt aus Liverpool.
b) Er hat einen Bruder.
c) Er möchte wissen: Hast du Geschwister?
d) Er fragt: Woher kommst du?
e) Das ist Steve.

Merke dir die Sätze. Wenn du zwei Personen miteinander bekannt machen willst, wirst du sie immer wieder brauchen.

5
31/4

1 Where are these six things in Ben's room?

a) Listen and draw the things in the right place.

Höre dir erst einmal alles an, bevor du mit der Aufgabe anfängst. Du kannst den Text so oft hören, wie du willst.

Du kannst die Gegenstände entweder bunt anmalen oder das passende Wort darauf schreiben.

b) Listen again. What colour are the things in the room?

31/4

2 Match the sounds and the people.

6 **a)** Listen to the sounds and number the pictures.

7 **b)** Write the picture number next to the right sentence. Listen and check.

- Now it's your turn Dave! ☐
- Shhh Sherlock! ☐
- Oh no! That's our bus! ☐
- OK, let's play football. ☐
- That's a cool bike! ☐
- Hi! Is that you Holly? ☐

8
31/4

3 Tick ✓ the right pictures.

Listen to Holly, Olivia and Olivia's dad.

Höre dir zuerst das ganze Gespräch an, um das Wichtigste zu verstehen. Lies die Aufgaben dann gut durch, damit du weißt, worauf du achten sollst.

1. Who is in the garden?

a) ☐

b) ☐

c) ☐

2. What is new in Olivia's room?

a) ☐

b) ☐

c) ☐

3. Where are Holly's guinea pigs?

a) ☐

b) ☐

c) ☐

Unit 2
This is my school

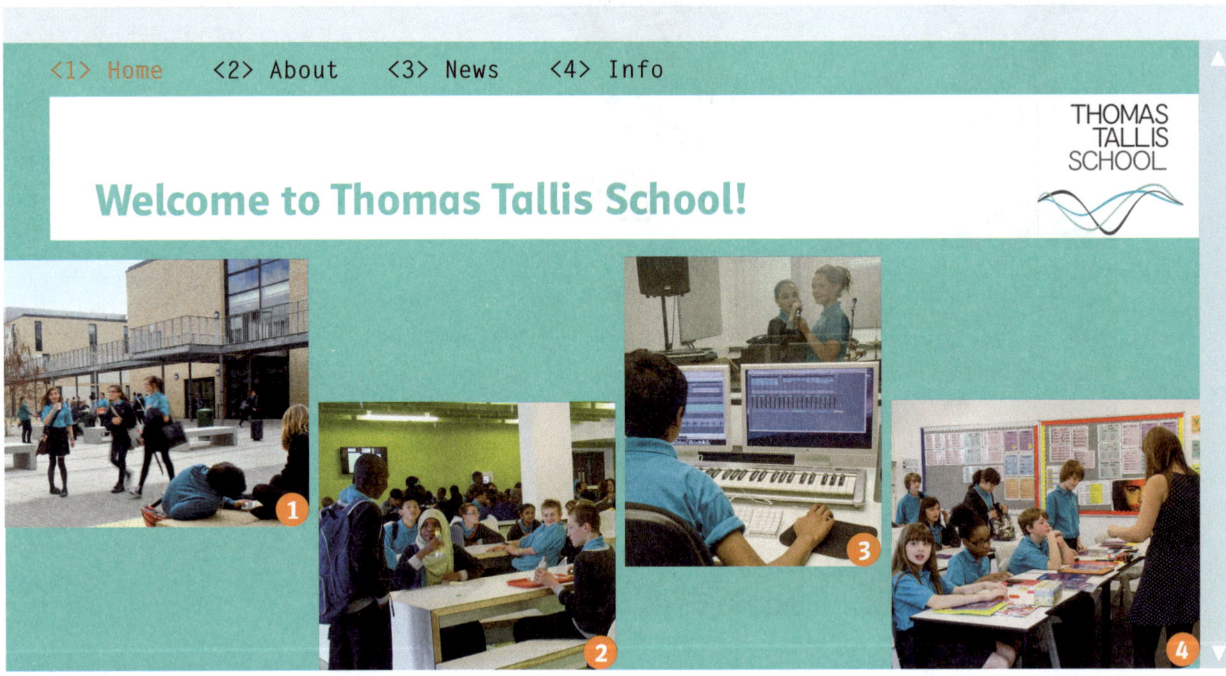

32/1

1 Put in the right words.

cafeteria | eat | talk | playground ✓
recording | sing | teacher | classroom

1. You can ______________ to your friends in the playground ______________.
2. You can ______________ food in the ______________.
3. You can ______________ in the TTS ______________ studio.
4. Mrs Bond is in the ______________. She's an English ______________.

33/3

2 (YOUR TURN) What's your favourite place in your school?

a) Draw a picture of your favourite place here.

b) Write about your favourite place.

My favourite place is ______________.

We can ______________ there.

I go there with ______________

______________.

1 What are the words?

34/3

a) Draw lines and make words.

1. tutor — studio
2. music — ground
3. play — fan
4. talent — book
5. recording — group
6. exercise — show

b) Write the words.

1. tutor group
2.
3.
4.
5.
6.

2 (LISTENING) What's in Dave's bag?

9
35/4

Listen to Dave and Luke. Tick ✓ the things in Dave's bag.

☐ 
☐ 
☐ 
☐ 
☐ 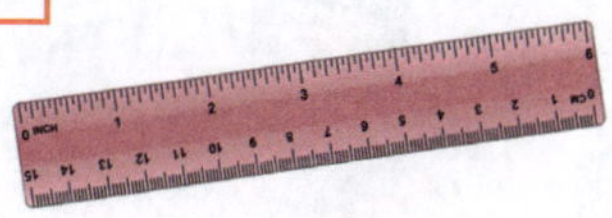
☐ 
☐ 

☐ 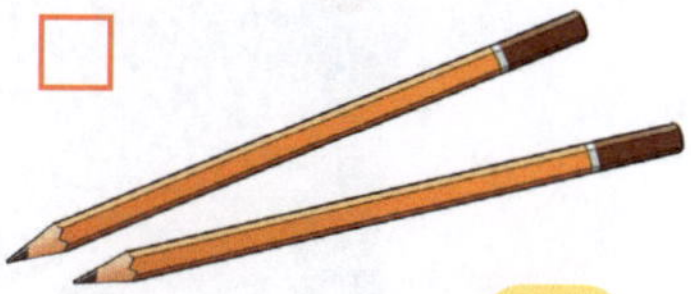

3 Find ten school words.

35/5

a) Find the words. (→ and ↓)

b) Write the words.

pen,

A	P	F	T	B	A	G	Y	E	J
U	E	N	L	S	K	X	I	E	H
K	N	B	P	R	U	L	E	R	R
B	S	O	V	M	Y	W	E	A	Z
T	E	A	C	H	E	R	Z	S	G
U	J	R	G	L	N	O	A	E	D
T	C	D	U	N	I	F	O	R	M
O	R	D	H	E	M	O	B	F	P
R	I	S	T	U	D	E	N	T	C
Q	C	A	R	E	T	A	K	E	R

4 Make sentences.

36/9

a) Draw lines.

Don't	play	+	the window.
	sing		the photo.
	write		that song.
	open		on the board.
	look at		football here.

b) Write the sentences in your exercise book.

5 (WRITING) Match the sentences with the pictures.

36/9

a) Write the right sentence under the picture.

- Don't play games here, please.
- Don't open that door. ✓
- Listen to the music.
- Don't sit down.
- Look at my new bag.
- Write your name here, please.

1

Don't open that door.

2

3

4

5

6

b) Write your sentences for the picture.

look at · open · eat

1. Mr Swindon: ______
2. Olivia: ______
3. Holly: ______

37/10

6 Finish Mr Swindon's sentences.

1. Open your bags and take out your books, please. (open)
2. Don't write on the board. (write)
3. ______ at the board, please. (look)
4. ______ the question, please. (read)
5. ______ in your exercise book. (write)
6. ______ in the classroom. (sing)
7. ______ on the table. (sit)

37/10

7 (MEDIATION) Read about the cafeteria.

Tick ✓ the right German sentences.

- Geht höflich und freundlich miteinander um. ☐
- Stellt euch zur Essensausgabe in einer Reihe an. ☐
- Bitte hier nicht singen. ☐
- Setzt euch zum Essen an einen Tisch. ☐
- Nehmt kein Geschirr oder Besteck mit. ☐
- Haltet die Tische sauber. ☐

Welcome to the TTS cafeteria!

Be nice to students and teachers.
You can talk here, but please don't sing.
Don't bring big bags into the cafeteria.
Sit at your table and eat there.
Don't play games in the cafeteria.
Don't make a mess on the tables, please.

37/11

8 (SPEAKING) Tell your partner.

a) Gebt euch gegenseitig Anweisungen und führt diese aus.

Example: Partner A: Open the window, please.
Partner B: Sit on the table.

Partner A: open the window ✓ | look at the board | take out your books | sing a song | take out your pens

Partner B: sit on the table ✓ | talk to me | write your name on the board | open your bag | go to the door

b) Findet weitere Anweisungen und führt diese aus.

1 (SOUNDS) Listen, write and say.

10 · 37/11

he · window · please · listen · it ✓ · dream

[ɪ]

1. [ɪt] it
2. [wɪndəʊ] ____________
3. [lɪsn] ____________

[i:]

4. [hi:] ____________
5. [dri:m] ____________
6. [pli:z] ____________

2 (SPEAKING) Make a dialogue.

37/11

a) Complete the dialogue.

Partner A: Are you new?

Partner B: Yes. I'm ________ Year 7.

Partner B: This school ________ big!

Partner A: Yes, ____________ very ____________.

Partner A: ________ Mr Green your tutor?

Partner B: Yes. He's nice. Is ____________ your tutor too?

Partner A: No, Mrs Dean ________ my tutor. ____________ nice too. Look, this is the cafeteria.

Partner B: Wow! ____________ cool!

Partner A: Yes. Let's eat!

Partner B: OK. We can sit there.

Partner A: No, let's ____________ next to the window.

Partner B: Great! Can you open the ______________, ____________?

Partner A: Yes, I can.

Partner B: Our school is cool!

b) Act the dialogue with a partner.

Versuche, die [ɪ]- und [i:]-Laute deutlich auszusprechen.

39/5 1 Write the days of the week.

a) Complete the days.

1. T _ _ S D A Y
2. S A _ _ _ D A Y
3. W E D _ _ _ D A Y
4. S U _ _ A Y
5. T _ _ _ _ D A Y
6. M _ _ _ A Y
7. _ _ I D A Y

b) Say the days in the right order. Start with Monday.

2 (LISTENING) Look at Olivia's timetable.

11 39/6

What is Olivia's favourite school day? Listen and tick ✓ the right day.

School timetable

	MON ☐	TUE ☐	WED ☐	THU ☐	FRI ☐
Registration					
Lesson 1	Maths	DT	Maths	French	English
Lesson 2	Art	Maths	PE	Science	Music
Break					
Lesson 3	English	French		Maths	Maths

Olivia's favourite school day is ____________________ .

3 (SPEAKING) School subjects

39/8

Spell the subjects for your partner. Write your partner's words in your exercise book.

Partner A

1. E – N – G – L – I – S – H
2. S – C – I – E – N – C – E
3. F – R – E – N – C – H

Partner B

1. M – A – T – H – S
2. T – E – C – H – N – O – L – O – G – Y
3. M – U – S – I – C

Decke die Buchstaben deiner Partnerin/deines Partners ab und höre ihr/ihm genau zu.

4 Fill in the chart.

41/10

Draw a picture of you and answer the questions.

Yes, she is. ✓	Yes, I am.	No, she isn't.
No, I'm not.	No, they aren't.	Yes, they are.

Olivia

1. Is she good at music?

   Yes, she is.

2. Is she new at TTS?

   ____

Jay, Dave and Luke

1. Are they from Germany?

   ____

2. Are they students at TTS?

   ____

You

1. Are you good at English?

   ____

2. Are you a football fan?

   ____

5 What does Dave say? Put in the right words.

41/11

1. ☹ Luke *isn't* my brother. — is / isn't ✓
2. ☺ ______________ Luke's friend. — I'm / I'm not
3. ☺ My favourite subject ______________ Design Technology. — is / isn't
4. ☹ ______________ good at French. It's not easy. — I'm / I'm not
5. ☺ I like my French teacher. Her jokes ______________ funny. — are / aren't
6. ☹ Luke's jokes ______________ funny. — are / aren't
7. ☹ Sherlock ______________ my pet. — is / isn't

41/11

6 (WRITING) Correct the sentences.

a) Use isn't or aren't.

1 Dave is ten.

Dave isn't ten.

2 The pencils are yellow.

3 Holly and Olivia are sisters.

4 Mrs Warren is a teacher.

b) Correct the sentences from a).

1. Dave is
2.
3.
4.

41/11

7 (WRITING) Write four sentences about Jay and Dave.

1. good at computer games • a good singer

2. good at Maths • good at Art

3 x 4 = 12

3. from Germany • from England

4. in the playground • in the classroom

1. Dave is good at computer games

but he isn't

2. Dave

but he

3. Jay and Dave

but they

4. Jay

1 Write sentences for the pictures.

42/2

A

B

C

D

A: Luke is good at football tricks.

B: ______________________

C: ______________________

D: ______________________

2 Complete the sentences.

42/2

restaurant	Indian
lunch ✓	tricks
saxophone	winner

1. The friends eat lunch __________ in the cafeteria.
2. Luke's football __________ are cool.
3. Olivia can play the __________.
4. Olivia is the __________ of the talent show.
5. "Let's go to the Indian __________."
6. Dave and Luke like __________ food.

1 (VIEWING) Match the headings (Überschriften) with the pictures.

45/2

- ☐ Jinsoo's school bag
- ☐ No chewing gum in bags!
- ☐ In the cafeteria
- ☐ In the Music room

A

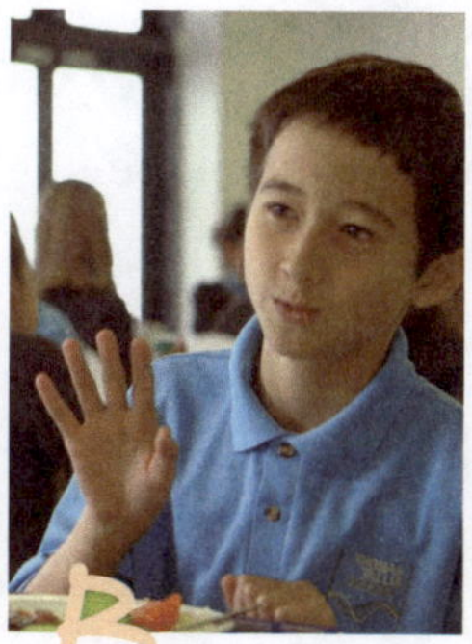
B

C

D

2 (VIEWING) Tick ✓ the right answers.

45/2

Bevor du den Film noch einmal anschaust, lies dir die Fragen durch.

1. Who is in the Music Club?
   - a) Laura ☐
   - b) Jinsoo ☐
   - c) Marley ☐

2. Who is in the Sign Language *(Zeichensprache)* Club?
   - a) Alicia ☐
   - b) Marley ☐
   - c) Jinsoo ☐

3. Who is in the cafeteria with Laura?
   - a) two boys ☐
   - b) two girls ☐
   - c) a girl ☐

4. Where is the chewing gum?
   - a) under Alicia's chair ☐
   - b) in Jinsoo's school bag ☐
   - c) in Laura's book ☐

3 A quiz

45/3

Spiele einen Schüler oder Lehrer aus dem Film nach, ohne dabei zu sprechen.
Deine Gruppe versucht zu erraten, wer du bist.

Zum Beispiel:
Are you a teacher? – Yes, I am. / No, I'm not.
Are you a … in the … Club? …

Ziel 1: Ich kann über meine Schule sprechen.

→ ⦾ wr82v2

Write sentences about your school.

board | playground | cafeteria | write | eat | play

There is a ________________ . We can ________________ games and talk there.

I ________________ in my exercise book. My teachers write on the ________________ .

My favourite place is the ________________ . We can ________________ there. I like the food.

6P

→ p. 32/1

Ziel 2: Ich kann Aufforderungen im Klassenzimmer verstehen und ausdrücken.

→ ⦾ 8fz9ya

a) Match the sentences with the numbers in the picture.

Don't write in my book. | Close the window, please.

Look at my new mobile. | Don't talk, please.

1. ________________
2. ________________
3. ________________
4. ________________

b) Look at the other students in the picture. What can the teacher say? Write four sentences.

- Don't write on the board.
- Listen to the students, please.
- Don't sing, please.
- Sit down, please.
- Don't dance here.
- Don't eat here.

5. ________________
6. ________________
7. ________________
8. ________________

8P

→ p. 32/2

Ziel 3: Ich kann sagen, was ich an der Schule mag oder nicht mag.

→ ⦾ 7n9mg9 → ⦾ u6z548

Read about Martin. What can he say?

"My favourite subject is ________________. ________________ isn't my favourite subject. My favourite day is ________________. We have ________________ and ________________. The ________________ are OK. Mr West is very ________________."

Martin
Favourite subject: Maths
(NOT English!!)
Favourite day: Thursday
(Maths and PE!)
Teachers: OK
(Mr West – VERY cool!)

7P
→ p. 32/3

Ziel 4: Ich kann eine Fotostory verstehen.

→ ⦾ zh3tm7

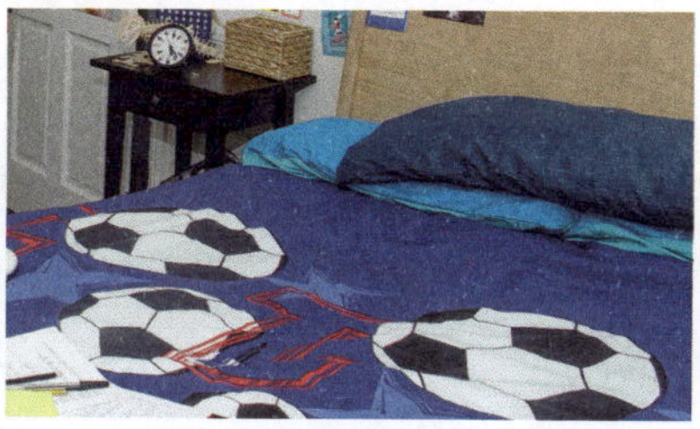

Right or wrong? Tick ✓ the right box.

	right	wrong
1. Luke can't find his bag.	☐	☐
2. Luke's mobile is on the bed.	☐	☐
3. Olivia is in the park.	☐	☐
4. Luke's mobile is in the park.	☐	☐

4P
→ p. 33/4

Ziel 5: Ich kann Informationen einer Schul-Website weitergeben.

Lies die Informationen über die AGs in der TTS und beantworte die Fragen auf Deutsch.

Music Club for Years 8 – 10	Monday	Music room
Music Club for Year 7	Tuesday	Music room
Girls' Football for Years 7 & 8	Wednesday	Playground
Science Club for Years 9 & 10	Thursday	Room 105

1. An welchen AGs können Holly und Olivia teilnehmen? ________________
2. Welche AG findet donnerstags statt? ________________
3. Wo spielen die Mädchen Fußball? ________________

3P
→ p. 33/5

Lösungen online
k684ah

Ziel 1: Ich kann über meine Schule sprechen.

Fülle die Lücken mit Informationen über deine Schule aus.
Sieh auf Seite 33 in deinem Buch nach, wenn du Hilfe brauchst.

Lerne die Sätze auswendig. Das ist hilfreich für die Klassenarbeit.

I go to ______________________. I'm in tutor group ______________. My tutor is ______________. My English teacher is ______________________. My favourite place is the ______________________. We can ______________ there. That's ______________.

Ziel 2: Ich kann Aufforderungen im Klassenzimmer ausdrücken und verstehen.

a) Welche Sätze drücken aus, dass du etwas tun sollst und welche, dass du etwas nicht tun sollst?

1. Open your exercise books, please. ☺
2. Don't talk, please. ☹
3. Don't take my eraser.
4. Open the window, please.
5. Write on the board, please.
6. Don't play with your mobile.
7. Read the question, please.
8. Don't play football here.

b) Schreibe nun selbst zwei Sätze.

Merke:
Aufforderungen: Look....
Verbote: Don't look....

1. ☹ in the classroom • sing

____

2. ☺ page 23 • look at • please

____

Ziel 3: Ich kann sagen, was ich in der Schule mag oder nicht mag.

a) Finde die Schulfächer in der Wortschlange.

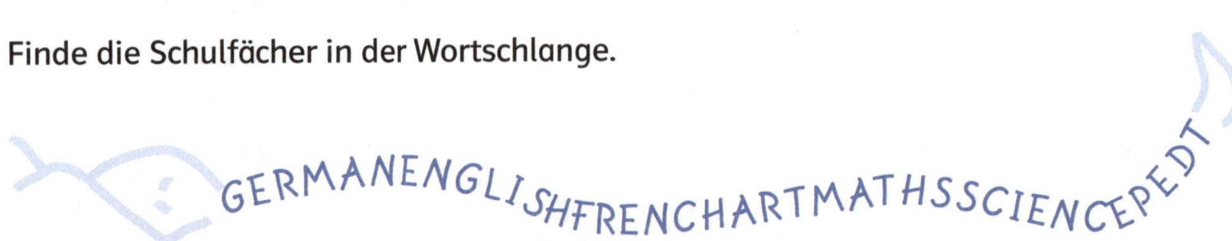

b) Schreibe auf, welches Fach du am liebsten magst und welches nicht.

My favourite subject is ______________. ______________ isn't my favourite subject.

Ziel 4: Ich kann eine Fotostory verstehen.

○ a) Sieh dir die Überschrift der Fotostory im Schülerbuch auf Seite 42 an: Welche Überschrift könnte noch zu der Fotostory passen?

1. In the cafeteria ☐ 2. The winner is … ☐ 3. A new timetable ☐

○ b) Welche Personen kommen in der Geschichte vor? Schreibe die Namen auf.

____

○ c) Ordne die Talente auf den Bildern den Personen zu:

1. It's _______________.

2. It's _______________.

3. It's _______________.

○ d) Wer nimmt nicht an der Talentshow teil? Setze einen Haken.

1. Olivia and Luke ☐ 2. Holly and Dave ☐

○ e) Wer gewinnt die Talentshow? Setze einen Haken.

 ☐
 ☐
 ☐

○ f) Warum denken Holly und Dave, dass entweder Jay oder Luke gewinnen wird?

1. Weil sie nicht wissen, dass Olivia auch teilnimmt. ☐
2. Weil sie denken, dass Olivia auf eine andere Schule geht. ☐

Ziel 5: Ich kann Informationen einer Schul-Website weitergeben.

○ a) Welche Wörter geben dir Informationen über die Cafeteria? Kreise sie ein.

lunchtime from 1.10 pm to 2.10 pm | pizza on Wednesdays | Girls' Football Club on Wednesday | Science Club on Thursday

○ b) Beantworte jetzt die Fragen.

1. Wann kann man in der Cafeteria essen?

____

2. Wann gibt es Pizza?

____

Suche immer erst nach Stichwörtern, bevor du versuchst, die Fragen zu beantworten.

51/3

1 Collect words for places in a school.

____

51/3

2 Read the text.

What can we do? Part I

It's lunch break at Thomas Tallis School. Jay, Dave and Luke are in the cafeteria.

Jay: Look! Here's Olivia, the talent star. You're a great saxophone player Olivia.
Olivia: Thanks Jay. You're good at music too. You're a good singer.
Jay: Yes, I love music. Can we go to the recording studio? We can sing and play instruments there.
Olivia: Yes, but a teacher must be there too. Let's go and see.
Luke: Great idea!

The students go to the recording studio but there's no teacher there.

Luke: What can we do now?
Jay: Let's go to the playground!
Olivia: Oh, no, we can't! It's time for Maths! Mr Swindon is in the classroom. Bye, boys!
Jay: Now, Luke, let's have fun!

Luke and Jay go to the playground.

Jay: This is cool! We can play basketball! Do you have a basketball?
Luke: No, I don't. Sorry.
Jay: Oh, look! What's that in the big old tree?
Luke: What? That black and white thing?
Jay: Yes! What is it? Is it a football? Or is it a cat?

51/3

3 Think about the story.

Um einen Text zu verstehen, hilft es, sich zu überlegen, wie die Geschichte weitergehen könnte.

a) Wie geht die Geschichte weiter? Was meinst du? Setze ein Häkchen unter das richtige Bild.

b) Schreibe in zwei bis drei Sätzen deine persönliche Fortsetzung der Geschichte auf Deutsch.

____

____

____

51/3

4 Read the text.

What can we do? Part II

Luke and Jay go to the big tree. There is a black and white cat in the tree.

Cat: Miaaaooooow! Miaaaooooow!
Luke: Hello, cat! What's the problem?
Jay: Look, it isn't happy.
Luke: How can we help? The tree is very big! That's a problem.
Cat: Miaaaooooow! Miaaaooooow!
Jay: We can ask Mrs Warren!

The boys go and find Mrs Warren. She is with Hannah from 7JD. Hannah is very unhappy.

Luke: Hey Hannah, are you OK?
Hannah: No, I'm not. I have a problem.
Jay: What's wrong?
Hannah: My cat … she isn't here!
Luke: Here? At school?
Hannah: Yes, she is here for the Science lesson.
Jay: Be cool! Mrs Warren, we need your ladder.

51/3

5 New words?

Lies die Geschichte noch einmal. Markiere die unbekannten Wörter und schreibe sie in die Tabelle.

Die unbekannten Wörter, die du nicht in die Tabelle einordnen kannst, solltest du im Wörterbuch nachschlagen.

Wörter und Phrasen, die ich aus dem Zusammenhang verstanden habe:	Wörter und Phrasen, die wie im Deutschen sind:	Wörter und Phrasen, die ähnlich wie ein schon bekanntes Wort sind:
______	______	______
______	______	______
______	______	______
______	______	______
______	______	______

51/3

6 Find the information in the text.

Ordne jedem Satz eine Farbe zu. Unterstreiche mit der jeweiligen Farbe die entsprechende Stelle im Text.

1. In the lunch break the friends are in the cafeteria. Zeilen ______
2. The students see no teacher at the recording studio. Zeilen ______
3. Olivia goes to the classroom. Zeilen ______
4. The boys see Mrs Warren with a girl. Zeilen ______
5. Hannah isn't happy. Zeile ____

Unit 3

My free time

1 Put in the right words.

52/1

at	music	play	school ✓	Saturdays
dad	On	practice	go	weekend

53/2

2 Make a mind map.

a) Put the words in the right places in the mind map.

computer games ✓ | music | netball | my team | the park | the cinema

free time

I play	I love	I go to
computer games	____________	____________
____________	____________	____________

b) Find more words for the mind map. Use the mind map and talk to your partner about your free time.

54/3

1 Find the names of the animals.

a) Write the names of the animals.

1. _ _ _ _ _ _ _
2. _ _ _ _ _ _ _ _
3. _ _ _ _ _ _ _
4. _ _ _ _ _

b) Find two zoo animals for each sentence.

1. They eat meat. ______
2. They are black and white. ______
3. They sleep a lot. ______
4. They come from India. ______

55/4

2 (WRITING) Make sentences about the animals.

a) Write sentences about the animals in your exercise book.

The tiger The elephant The snake	+ eats sleeps	+ eighteen hours a day. grass. for five months in winter. meat. small animals. four hours a day.

b) Check your sentences with the animal information on page 54 in your book.

12
55/5

3 (LISTENING) Listen to the numbers.

Put a circle ◯ around the right number.

1. 25 52
2. 74 47
3. 67 76
4. 46 64
5. 94 49
6. 38 83
7. 30 13
8. 15 50

55/6

4 A quiz

Schreibe deiner Partnerin / deinem Partner mit deinem Finger eine zweistellige Zahl auf ihren / seinen Rücken. Sie / Er errät die Zahl. Wechselt euch ab.

56/10

5 Choose the right verb and complete the sentences.

1. The students _love_ the animals at the ~~zoo~~. (love / loves)
2. The elephants ________ grass. (eat / eats)
3. The small elephant ________ fruit too. (love / loves)
4. Lizzie, the snake, ________ mice. Yuck! (eat / eats)
5. The monkeys ________ fruit. (eat / eats)
6. My favourite monkey ________ grass too! (love / loves)

Ein 's' ist genug:
The students love the animals at the zoo.
The student loves the animals at the zoo.

56/10

6 Put in the right form of the verb.

go | eat | play | say ✓ | sleep | work

1. Fred _says_ , "Hello!" to Edgar.
2. The tigers ________ meat for lunch.
3. Fred ________ at the zoo.
4. The animals ________ in the zoo.
5. Mick, the monkey, ________ with a football.
6. On Saturdays people ________ to the zoo.

56/12

7 Finish the sentences.

works on the computer | go to the zoo | cleans the cages | works at the zoo ✓ | like the zoo and the animals | likes the tigers | talks to Edgar

Fred _works at the zoo_ . He often ________ but sometimes he ________ . On Saturdays his friends Emma and Danny ________ . Emma ________ , the elephant. Danny ________ . Emma and Danny ________ .

57/13

8 Write about the animals.

1. Bats _don't like_ bananas.
2. Tigers ________ fruit.
3. Mice ________ at night.
4. Snakes ________ .

don't eat | don't sleep | don't like ✓ | don't walk

9 What do Tom and Peter do? Finish the sentences.

57/13

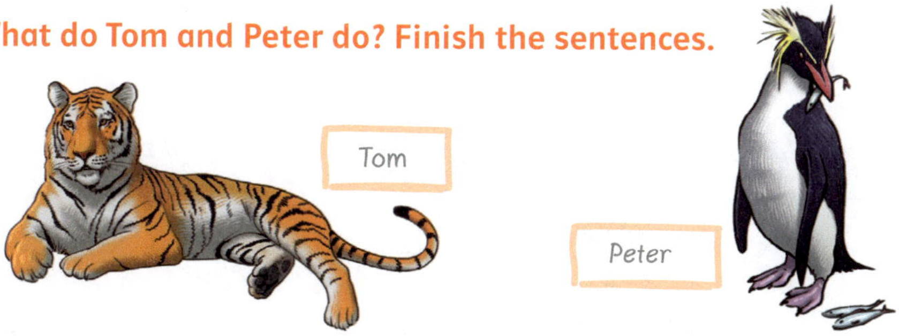

1. Tom sleeps a lot. Peter _doesn't sleep_ a lot.
2. Tom eats big animals. Peter ______ big animals. He eats fish.
3. Tom comes from India. Peter ______ from India. He comes from Africa.
4. Tom plays with other tigers. Peter ______ with tigers. He plays with penguins.
5. Tom runs 40 kilometres an hour. Peter ______. He swims in the water.

10 What's right: don't or doesn't?

57/14

a) Put in the right word and put a circle ◯ around the right letter.

	doesn't	don't
1. Parrots _don't_ live in water.	Z	(M)
2. Edgar, the elephant, ______ eat meat.	O	A
3. Tom, the tiger, ______ come from Germany.	N	R
4. Penguins ______ live in trees.	U	K
5. Fred ______ sleep at the zoo.	E	I
6. Fred says, "I ______ work at night."	T	Y

b) Look at the letters in the circles ◯ in a). What's the animal? It's a ______.

11 (YOUR TURN) What's my animal?

57/15

Say three things about an animal. Your partner guesses the animal. Take turns.

Example:
Lena: My animal lives in … . It eats … . It likes … .
Lukas: It's a …!
Lena: No, that's wrong. / Yes, that's right.
Lukas: Is your animal a …?
Lena: Yes, that's right.

57/15

1 (SOUNDS) [z] and [s]

13

a) Listen and write the words.

listen | music | famous | numbers | zoo ✓ | seventy

1. [zu:] zoo
2. ['mju:zɪk] ____________
3. ['nʌmbəz] ____________

4. ['sevntɪ] ____________
5. ['lɪsn] ____________
6. ['feɪməs] ____________

14

b) Listen to this sentence. Put a circle ◯ around the [z] and [s] sounds.

On Saturdays Luke goes to the cinema with his famous sister.

57/15

2 (SPEAKING) Make a dialogue.

a) Complete the dialogue.

Saturday | school | Sunday | zoo | tennis | cinema | let's ✓ | See | music | science fiction

Partner A

Hi, let's ____________ watch a movie at the weekend.

Partner B

Hi! I can't go on ____________, I have ____________ practice.

Partner A

Oh! I can't go on ____________, I play ____________.

Partner B

And Friday? Let's go to the cinema on Friday, after ____________.

Partner A

What movie can we watch?

Partner B

We can watch a ____________ movie.

Partner A

Yes, that's cool! We can go to the new ____________ next to the ____________.

Partner B

Great! ____________ you on Friday.

Partner A

Bye!

b) Act the dialogue with a partner.

Versuche, die [z]- und [s]-Laute deutlich auszusprechen.

1 (READING) Read about Fred's busy Saturday in your book again.

58/1

Put the sentences in the right order.

- He feeds Edgar. ☐
- He works on the computer. ☐
- Fred gets up. 1
- He cleans the cages. ☐
- He has breakfast. ☐
- He feeds the other animals. ☐
- He goes to the zoo. ☐

2 Write about the monkey's day.

58/1

clean | feeds | breakfast | dirty | early ✓ | fruit | afternoon

"I get up *early* – at six o'clock. Fred ______ Edgar at seven o'clock. Then he comes with ______ for me. That's my ______ . In the ______ Fred ______ my cage. But it isn't a mess. I'm not a ______ animal."

3 (LISTENING) What time is it?

15
58/3

Listen and tick ✓ the right answers.

1. 10.08 ☐ 8.10 ☐
2. 6.55 ☐ 6.05 ☐
3. 11.40 ☐ 11.14 ☐
4. 5.24 ☐ 4.25 ☐

4 (LISTENING) Draw the times.

16
59/5

a) Listen and draw the times.

b) Draw four times for your partner. Then your partner says the times.

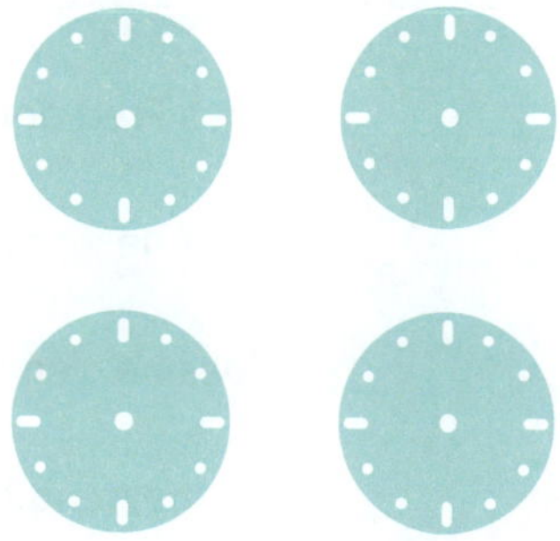

5 Make questions and answers.

60/9

In der 3. Person Singular bildest du Fragen mit Does …, sonst mit Do … .

a) Put in Do or Does.

1. Does Fred like his work?
2. ______ Fred have breakfast at the zoo?
3. ______ the animals have dirty cages?
4. ______ Fred work a lot?
5. ______ the penguins eat bananas?

b) Answer the questions from a).

1. Yes, he does.
2. ______
3. ______
4. ______
5. ______

6 Make questions about Holly and her pets.

60/9

Lies zuerst die Antworten. Sie helfen dir, die Fragen zu bilden.

1. Does Holly ______ – Yes, Holly loves animals.
2. ______ – Yes, she goes to the zoo on Sundays.
3. ______ – Yes, she plays with her pets.
4. Do the guinea pigs ______ – Yes, they live in a cage.
5. ______ – Yes, they like fruit.
6. ______ – Yes, they play with Holly.

7 Put in the right question word.

61/10

1. ______ does Fred get up? – At six o'clock. (When / Where)
2. ______ does he work? – At the zoo. (What / Where)
3. ______ does he clean? – The cages. (Where / What)
4. ______ do the penguins sleep? – At night. (Where / When)

61/11

8 Make questions.

Nummeriere zuerst die Satzteile. Schreibe dann die Fragen auf.

1. does (2) • football (5) • Luke (3) • where (1) • play (4)

   Where does Luke play football ?

2. TV (__) • when (__) • Jay and Dave (__) • do (__) • watch (__)

   ______________________________ ?

3. Holly (__) • want (__) • does (__) • what (__)

   ______________________________ ?

4. to the cinema (__) • go (__) • Dave (__) • on Mondays (__) • does (__)

   ______________________________ ?

17
61/12

9 (LISTENING) Listen to Jay's interview with the singer Ashraf.

Look at the pictures of Ashraf. What does Ashraf do? Tick ✓ the right pictures.

1 

2 

3 

4 

5 

61/12

10 Write the questions in English.

a) Carola und ihre kleine Schwester Linda machen Urlaub in Greenwich. Sie treffen Olivia im Park. Linda bittet Carola, Olivia einige Fragen auf Englisch zu stellen, da sie noch kein Englisch kann.

1. Was machst du in deiner Freizeit? – ______________ do in your free time?
2. Wohin gehst du mit deinen Freunden? – ______________ go with your friends?
3. Wann gehst du ins Kino? – ______________ go to the cinema?
4. Gehst du in den Zoo? – ______________ go to the zoo?

b) Stelle nun deiner Partnerin / deinem Partner die Fragen aus a) auf Englisch. Sie / Er antwortet dir. Wechselt euch ab.

1 Find the right words.

62/2

café | nuts | police officer | raccoon

1. ______________

2. ______________

3. ______________

4. ______________

2 (READING) Put the sentences in the right order.

62/2

They find the hole and the nuts. ☐

Luke and Sherlock go to the café. [1]

Luke and Sherlock look for clues. ☐

The police officer can see raccoons. ☐

Mrs Abrihim talks to the police officer about the mess. ☐

The ladder is in the kitchen. ☐

3 (READING) Right or wrong? Tick ✓ the right box.

62/2

	right	wrong
1. Luke and Sherlock play with Dave in the park.	☐	☐
2. They see Mrs Abrihim and the police officer at the café.	☐	☐
3. There is a mess in Mrs Abrihim's café every day.	☐	☐
4. Luke and Sherlock look around the café for their football.	☐	☐
5. Sherlock looks in the hole.	☐	☐

4 (WRITING) What do Luke and Sherlock do next in the story?

62/3

Draw a picture and write two or three sentences.

Luke and Sherlock ______________

____

____

____

____

____

____

65/2

1 (VIEWING) Match the things with the right people.

65/2

2 (VIEWING) Tick ✓ the right answers.

1. What does Marley want to do at the weekend?
   a) go to the cinema ☐
   b) go to the park ☐
   c) sing ☐

2. What does Alicia say to Laura?
   a) Bye! ☐
   b) Thanks. ☐
   c) That's my book. ☐

3. What does Marley feed?
   a) his dog ☐
   b) his cat ☐
   c) his fish ☐

4. Who listens to music?
   a) Marley ☐
   b) Jinsoo ☐
   c) Laura ☐

5. Where do the friends go on Saturday?
   a) to school ☐
   b) to the park ☐
   c) to Laura's house ☐

6. Who has the football in the park?
   a) Jinsoo ☐
   b) Marley ☐
   c) Laura ☐

65/2

3 Questions for Marley

a) What can you ask Marley? Write questions in your exercise book.

When do you	get up	…?
Where do you	like	…?
What do you	play	breakfast?
Do you	have	a pet?

b) Find the answers in the film and write them in your exercise book.

3 Checkpoint

Ziel 1: Ich kann über meine Freizeit sprechen.

→ ◎ e742ap

Look at the pictures. What does Jayden do in his free time? Write four sentences.

help | listen to | play ✓ | watch

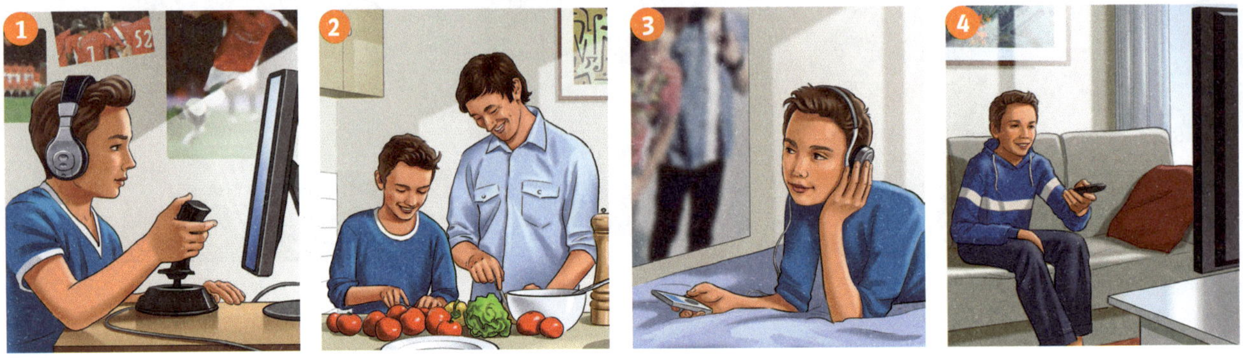

1. He plays computer games.
2. ______________________
3. ______________________
4. ______________________

3P

→ p. 48/1

Ziel 2: Ich kann ein Tier vorstellen.

→ ◎ 4vz2c7

Write an animal profile.

This is Johnny________, the ____________. He is ________

____________. He ______________, but he ________

______________. Johnny ______________

____________. He ______________

____________. He ______________

____________.

name: Johnny
animal: giraffe
age: 15
eats: plants :-) meat :-(

other information:
* 5 metres high
* sleeps three hours a day
* runs 50 kilometres an hour

7P

→ p. 48/2

Ziel 3: Ich kann über meinen Alltag sprechen.

→ ◎ 6nj388 → ◎ nm67d5

What does Jaden say about his day?

7:00 get up ✓
7:30 have breakfast
8:20 walk to school
4:45 play with my pets

1. I get up at seven o'clock.
2. I have ______________________
3. I walk ______________________
4. I play ______________________

3P

→ p. 48/3

Ziel 4: Ich kann eine Detektivgeschichte verstehen.

→ ⦾ vm9re9

Where are the bananas?

It's four o'clock. Olivia and Claire are in the kitchen.

Olivia: Can I have a banana please, Claire?

Claire: Yes, there are four bananas on the table. – Oh! Where are they?

Olivia: I don't know.

Now it's 5:30. Olivia can't find her red T-shirt.

Claire: Isn't it in your room?

Olivia: No, it isn't there. Hm. Does Lucy have it? She takes my things …

But Olivia's T-shirt isn't with Lucy's things.

At six o'clock Olivia sees Lucy in the garden. She has a red T-shirt – Olivia's red T-shirt! Olivia goes into the garden. Lucy puts the red T-shirt on the grass – next to four bananas!

Olivia: What's that, Lucy?

Lucy: It's a home for mice. They can live there. I want mice as pets!

Olivia: But mice don't want T-shirts. They make a home with grass. And they eat nuts, not bananas.

The girls get nuts from the kitchen and Lucy puts the nuts under a tree.

Read the story. Then tick ✓ the right box.

	right	wrong
1. There are four bananas in the kitchen.	☐	☐
2. Olivia sees Lucy in the garden at 5:30.	☐	☐
3. Olivia's red T-shirt is in the garden.	☐	☐
4. Mice eat grass and T-shirts.	☐	☐
5. Now mice can eat nuts in Lucy's garden.	☐	☐

5P

→ p. 49/4

Ziel 5: Ich kann Informationen über Schul-AGs weitergeben.

Deine jüngere Schwester sieht sich mit dir diese Webseite an. Beantworte ihre Fragen auf Deutsch.

INTERNET

<1> Home <2> About <3> News <4> Info

TTS Dance Club

Do you like dancing? We want new dancers!

You can't dance? No problem. You can learn with us!
Every year we put on a show for friends and parents.

Dance practice: lunchtime on Tuesdays
after school on Thursdays

1. Muss man schon tanzen können? ______________________
2. Treten die Tänzer auch öffentlich auf? ______________________
3. Wann proben sie? ______________________

3P

→ p. 49/5

Lösungen online
v4bx7i

Ziel 1: Ich kann über meine Freizeit sprechen.

○ a) Welche Wörter passen zusammen? Ziehe Verbindungslinien.

play | go to | listen to | help | watch | go to | watch

the zoo | football | movies | TV | music | the cinema | my family

○ b) Was machst du in deiner Freizeit? Schreibe zwei Aktivitäten auf.

In my free time I play ______________________ and I __________________________________ too.

○ Ziel 2: Ich kann ein Tier vorstellen.

Sieh dir die Bilder an und vervollständige die Sätze.

1. The monkey comes ______________________ from India.
2. The elephant ______________________ grass.
3. The snake ______________________ for five months in winter.
4. The tiger ______________________ a lot.
5. The penguin ______________________ water.

He, she, it –
das -s muss mit!

Ziel 3: Ich kann über meinen Alltag sprechen.

○ a) Was macht Fred jeden Tag? Verbinde die Aktivitäten und Uhrzeiten.

7:00 | 3:10 | 6:30 | 1:15 | 6:00 ✓

clean the cages | walk to the zoo | have lunch | have breakfast | get up ✓

○ b) Schreibe auf, was Fred macht.

Fred gets up at 6 o'clock. He ______________________

____

____

G2 Mit G sind die Grammatikkapitel gekennzeichnet und der Reihe nach durchnummeriert.

G1 Language tip: Die Seiten kennzeichnen zusätzliche Grammatikkapitel.
Du kannst dir die neuen Formen dort wie neue Vokabeln merken oder – wenn du es genau wissen willst – ein paar Regeln dazu lernen.

G1 Language tip: Besitzangaben mit 's

The possessive form with 's

Wenn du sagen willst, zu wem etwas gehört, hängst du **'s an die Person.**

Lucy's sister	Lucys Schwester
Dave's cat	Daves Katze
Kate's mum	Kates Mama
Rob's brother	Robs Bruder
my **mother's** father	der Vater meiner Mutter
my **friend's** football	der Fußball meines Freundes

Achtung, wenn mehreren Personen etwas gehört und bereits ein **s am Wortende** steht. Vergleiche:

my **brother's** room	das Zimmer meines Bruders (ein Bruder)
Aber: my **brothers'** room	das Zimmer meiner Brüder (mehrere Brüder)

Im Deutschen kannst du Besitzangaben unterschiedlich ausdrücken. Vergleiche:

Sherlock is **Luke's** dog.	Sherlock ist Lukes Hund. Sherlock ist der Hund von Luke.

Im Deutschen gibt es kein Häkchen (Apostroph) vor dem s.

G2 Das Verb be (Aussagen)

The verb be (statements)

Das Verb **be** (sein) hat verschiedene Formen: **am**, **are** und **is**.
Es gibt Langformen und Kurzformen.

I **am**	**I'm**	ich bin
you **are**	**you're**	du bist / Sie sind
he **is**	**he's**	er ist
she **is**	**she's**	sie ist
it **is**	**it's**	es ist
we **are**	**we're**	wir sind
you **are**	**you're**	ihr seid / Sie sind
they **are**	**they're**	sie sind

Beim Schreiben verwendest du meistens Langformen und beim Sprechen Kurzformen.

G3 Language tip: Der Plural

The plural

Möchtest du von Dingen oder Personen in der **Mehrzahl** (Plural) sprechen, hängst du in den meisten Fällen einfach ein **-s** an.

one book, seven **books**	ein Buch, sieben Bücher
one CD, five **CDs**	eine CD, fünf CDs
one mobile, two **mobiles**	ein Handy, zwei Handys

Bei Nomen, die auf einen **Zischlaut** enden, zum Beispiel **box**, hängst du in der Mehrzahl ein **-es** an.

There are three **boxes** on the table.	Drei Schachteln sind auf dem Tisch.

Die meisten Nomen, die auf **-y** enden, sehen im Plural so aus:

one family, two families	eine Familie, zwei Familien
Aber: one boy, two boys	ein Junge, zwei Jungen

Manche Nomen haben unregelmäßige Pluralformen.

one shelf, two **shelves**	ein Regal, zwei Regale

G4 Fragen mit be

Questions with be

Fragen, auf die man mit Ja oder Nein antworten kann, bildest du so:

Am I late?	Bin ich zu spät?
Is Holly from Greenwich?	Ist Holly aus Greenwich?
Are you at home?	Bist du zu Hause? Seid ihr zu Hause?
Are Sherlock and Sid guinea pigs?	Sind Sherlock und Sid Meerschweinchen?

Bei Fragen mit Fragewörtern steht das Fragewort immer am Satzanfang.

Who is Holly?	Wer ist Holly?
Where are Fluff and Honey?	Wo sind Fluff und Honey?
What is under the bed?	Was ist unter dem Bett?

Who? = Wer?
Where? = Wo?

G5 Language tip: Der Artikel: a, an und the

The article: a, an and the

Der **unbestimmte Artikel** (ein, eine) heißt im Englischen **a** oder **an.**
Beginnt das folgende Wort mit einem **Konsonanten**, sagt man **a**.
Beginnt das folgende Wort mit einem **Vokal**, sagt man **an**.

a [ə] **bag**	eine Tasche	**an** [ən] **exercise book**	ein Heft

Der **bestimmte Artikel** (der, die, das) heißt im Englischen immer **the**.
Beginnt das folgende Wort mit einem **Konsonanten**, sagt man **[ðə]**.
Beginnt das folgende Wort mit einem **Vokal**, sagt man **[ði]**.

Vokale sind a, e, i, o, u. Alle anderen Buchstaben sind Konsonanten.

the [ðə] bag	die Tasche	**the [ði]** exercise book	das Heft

Auch wenn **u** ein Vokal ist, steht vor Wörtern wie **uniform** ein **a**. Achte auf die Aussprache.

a uniform [ə ˈjuːnɪfɔːm]	eine Uniform

G6 Der Imperativ

The imperative

Der Imperativ ist die **Befehlsform**. So forderst du jemanden auf, etwas zu tun:

Open the window, please. **Be** quiet.	Öffne das Fenster, bitte. Sei still.

So forderst du jemanden auf, etwas **nicht** zu tun:

Don't look in your books. **Don't be** late, please.	Schaut nicht in eure Bücher. Sei bitte nicht zu spät.

G7 Die Verneinung von be

The negative of be

So bildest du die **Verneinung** mit **be**. Es gibt Langformen und Kurzformen.

I **am not**	I'**m not**	ich bin nicht
you **are not**	you **aren't**	du bist nicht / Sie sind nicht
he / she / it **is not**	he / she / it **isn't**	er / sie / es ist nicht
we **are not**	we **aren't**	wir sind nicht
you **are not**	you **aren't**	ihr seid nicht / Sie sind nicht
they **are not**	they **aren't**	sie sind nicht

Beim Schreiben verwendest du meistens Langformen und beim Sprechen Kurzformen.

Beim Schreiben verwendest du meistens Langformen und beim Sprechen Kurzformen.
Du kannst Fragen mit Kurzantworten beantworten:

Am I late? / **Are we** late?	Yes, **you are.**	No, **you aren't.**
Are you at home?	Yes, **I am / we are.**	No, **I'm not / we aren't.**
Is Dave / Holly / it from Greenwich?	Yes, **he / she / it is.**	No, **he / she / it isn't.**
Are Sherlock and Sid guinea pigs?	Yes, **they are.**	No, **they aren't.**

G8 Die einfache Gegenwart: Aussagen

The simple present: statements

Wenn du über **Gewohnheiten** oder Dinge sprichst, die **allgemein gültig** sind, verwendest du die einfache Gegenwart.

I	**play**	ich spiele
you	**play**	du spielst / Sie spielen
he / she / it	**plays**	er / sie / es spielt
we	**play**	wir spielen
you	**play**	ihr spielt / Sie spielen
they	**play**	sie spielen

Signalwörter

on Mondays	montags
every day	jeden Tag
always	immer

Bei Verben mit Zischlaut wie **watch**, **finish**, **guess**, hängst du bei **he**, **she**, **it** ein **-es** an.

Luke **watches** [ɪz] TV every Saturday.	Luke sieht jeden Samstag fern.

Manche Verben haben unregelmäßige Formen bei **he**, **she**, **it.**

I **have** → he **has**   I **go** → she **goes** [gəʊz]   I **do** → he **does** [dʌz]

G9 Die einfache Gegenwart: Verneinung

The simple present: negatives

Mit **don't** (= do not) oder **doesn't** (= does not) vor einem Verb kannst du sagen, was man **nicht** macht. So bildest du die Verneinung:

I	**don't**	play	ich spiele nicht
you	**don't**	play	du spielst nicht / Sie spielen nicht
he / she / it	**doesn't**	play	er / sie / es spielt nicht
we	**don't**	play	wir spielen nicht
you	**don't**	play	ihr spielt nicht / Sie spielen nicht
they	**don't**	play	sie spielen nicht

G10 Die einfache Gegenwart: Fragen

The simple present: questions

Bei **Fragen mit Vollverben**, auf die man mit Ja oder nein antworten kann, steht immer **do** oder **does** am Satzanfang.

Do	I	**have** …?	Habe ich …?
Do	you	**have** …?	Hast du …? / Haben Sie …?
Does	he	**have** …?	Hat er …?
Does	she	**have** …?	Hat sie …?
Does	it	**have** …?	Hat es …?
Do	we	**have** …?	Haben wir …?
Do	you	**have** …?	Habt ihr …? / Haben Sie …?
Do	they	**have** …?	Haben sie …?

Bei Fragen mit Fragewörtern steht das Fragewort immer am Satzanfang.

What do you **do** on Mondays?	Was machst du montags?
Where do they **meet**?	Wo treffen sie sich?
When does Holly **eat** breakfast?	Wann frühstückt Holly?
Why does Fred **work** at the zoo?	Warum arbeitet Fred im Zoo?

G11 Language tip: Personalpronomen und Possessivbegleiter

Personal pronouns and possessive determiners

Pronomen stehen **für** ein anderes Nomen, z. B. **the boy** → **he**, **the girl** → **she** usw.
Personalpronomen haben eine Subjektform und eine Objektform.
Possessivbegleiter drücken aus, wem oder zu wem etwas gehört.

Personalpronomen Subjektform		Objektform		**Possessivbegleiter** (Besitzform)	
I	ich	me	mir / mich	my	mein(e)
you	du / Sie	you	dir / dich / Ihnen / Sie	your	dein(e) / Ihr(e)
he	er	him	ihm / ihn	his	sein(e)
she	sie	her	ihr / sie	her	ihr(e)
it	es	it	ihm / es	its	sein(e)
we	wir	us	uns	our	unser(e)
you	ihr / Sie	you	euch / Ihnen / Sie	your	euer(e) / Ihr(e)
they	sie	them	ihnen / sie	their	ihr(e)

It steht im Englischen für alle Dinge. Im Deutschen ist das nicht so. Vergleiche:

the pen → **It** is blue.	der Stift → **Er** ist blau.
the bag → **It** is nice. I like **it**.	die Tasche → **Sie** ist schön. Ich mag **sie**.
the house → **It** is old.	das Haus → **Es** ist alt.

G12 Die Wortstellung im Satz
Word order

Die wichtigste Wortstellungsregel in englischen Aussagesätzen lautet: **Subjekt – Verb – Objekt.**

Subjekt	Verb	Objekt	
I	like	parties.	Ich mag Partys.
Olivia	has	a cool costume.	Olivia hat ein cooles Kostüm.
Honey and Fluff	eat	grass.	Honey und Fluff essen Gras.

Wenn du sagen möchtest, wie oft etwas passiert, kannst du **Häufigkeitsadverbien** (adverbs of frequency) benutzen. Sie stehen im Englischen **vor dem Verb**. Vergleiche:

Mum	**always**	**makes** a cake for us.	Mama macht immer einen Kuchen für uns.
Jay	**often**	**has** a party.	Jay macht oft eine Party.
My friends	**never**	**forget** my birthday.	Meine Freunde vergessen nie meinen Geburtstag.

In Sätzen mit **be** steht das Adverb **dahinter**.

Mr Swindon **is never** late. — Mr Swindon kommt nie zu spät.

G13 Die einfache Vergangenheit: Aussagen
The simple past: statements

Um über Dinge zu sprechen, die in der **Vergangenheit** passiert und **vorbei** sind, verwendest du im Englischen die einfache Vergangenheit (simple past).

Signalwörter
- **yesterday** – gestern
- **last week** – letzte Woche

Bei den meisten Verben hängst du für das **simple past** die Endung **-ed** an das Verb. Sie ist für alle Personen gleich. Im Deutschen gibt es zwei Möglichkeiten, Vergangenes auszudrücken.

I **played** netball.	Ich spielte Netzball. / Ich habe Netzball gespielt.
You **watched** TV yesterday.	Du sahst gestern fern.
He **walked** on the beach.	Er lief am Strand. / Er ist am Strand gelaufen.
She **worked** last weekend.	Sie arbeitete letztes Wochenende.
We **talked** to Ray-B last week.	Wir sprachen letzte Woche mit Ray-B.
They **wanted** to buy things.	Sie wollten Sachen kaufen.

Achtung Aussprache:
wanted [ˈwɒntɪd]

Achtung Schreibweise:
stop → stopped [stɒpt]

Einige Verben haben unregelmäßige Formen.

go → **went**	see → **saw**
buy → **bought**	have → **had**
do → **did**	win → **won**

G14 Die einfache Vergangenheit: Fragen

The simple past: questions

Du kennst bereits Fragen mit **do** und **does**. Für **Fragen in der Vergangenheit**, auf die man mit ja oder nein antworten kann, steht immer **did** am Satzanfang.

Did	I	**have** …?	Hatte ich …?
Did	you	**have** …?	Hattest du …? / Hatten Sie …?
Did	he	**have** …?	Hatte er …?
Did	she	**have** …?	Hatte sie …?
Did	it	**have** …?	Hatte es …?
Did	we	**have** …?	Hatten wir …?
Did	you	**have** …?	Hattet ihr …? / Hatten Sie …?
Did	they	**have** …?	Hatten sie …?

Bei Fragen mit Fragewörtern steht das Fragewort immer am Satzanfang.

What (was)	**did**	you	**do**?
Where (wo)	**did**	he	**go**?
When (wann)	**did**	she	**eat**?
Why (warum)	**did**	we	**walk**?
How (wie)	**did**	they	**go** there?

G15 Language tip: Modale Hilfsverben: can / can't, must und needn't

Modal auxiliaries: can / can't, must and needn't

Modale Hilfsverben sind z. B. **can**, **can't**, **must** und **needn't**.
Sie kommen immer zusammen mit einem anderen Verb vor.

I	**must**	**stop** now.	Ich **muss** jetzt aufhören.
He	**can't**	**go** now.	Er **kann** jetzt **nicht** gehen.
She	**needn't**	**do** it.	Sie **muss** es **nicht** machen.
We	**can**	**help** you.	Wir **können** dir helfen.
They	**needn't**	**be** sad.	Sie **müssen nicht** traurig sein.

Fragen mit **can** oder **must** bildest du so:

Can you **help** me, please?	Kannst du mir bitte helfen?
Must I **go** now?	Muss ich jetzt gehen?
What can we **do**?	Was können wir tun?

G16 Die einfache Vergangenheit von be

The simple past of be

Das Verb **be** hat in der Vergangenheit zwei verschiedene Formen: **was** und **were**. Für die **Verneinung** setzt du einfach **not** dahinter. Es gibt dabei Langformen und Kurzformen.

I **was**	ich war	I **was not**	I **wasn't**	ich war nicht
you **were**	du warst / Sie waren	you **were not**	you **weren't**	du warst nicht
he **was**	er war	he **was not**	he **wasn't**	er war nicht
she **was**	sie war	she **was not**	she **wasn't**	sie war nicht
it **was**	es war	it **was not**	it **wasn't**	es war nicht
we **were**	wir waren	we **were not**	we **weren't**	wir waren nicht
you **were**	ihr wart / Sie waren	you **were not**	you **weren't**	ihr wart nicht
they **were**	sie waren	they **were not**	they **weren't**	sie waren nicht

Bei **Fragen**, die man mit Ja oder Nein beantworten kann, steht **was** oder **were** am Satzanfang. Du kannst diese Fragen mit Kurzantworten beantworten.

Was Sid at home?	Yes, **he was**.	No, **he wasn't**.
Were they at Highfield Farm?	Yes, **they were**.	No, **they weren't**.

Bei Fragen mit Fragewörtern steht das Fragewort am Satzanfang. Darauf folgt **was** oder **were**.

Where was Sid at the weekend? **When were** they at Highfield Farm?

G17 Die einfache Vergangenheit: Verneinung

The simple past: negatives

Du kennst schon die Verneinung für die Gegenwart mit **don't** und **doesn't**. Um zu sagen, was in der Vergangenheit nicht passiert ist, setzt du **didn't** vor das Verb.

Signalwörter

last Monday	letzten Montag
last week	letzte Woche
yesterday	gestern

I	**didn't go**	ich ging nicht
you	**didn't go**	du gingst nicht / Sie gingen nicht
he	**didn't go**	er ging nicht
she	**didn't go**	sie ging nicht
it	**didn't go**	es ging nicht
we	**didn't go**	wir gingen nicht
you	**didn't go**	ihr gingt nicht / Sie gingen nicht
they	**didn't go**	sie gingen nicht

Das Verb nach **didn't** steht immer in der **Grundform**. Vergleiche:

We **went** to the farm last weekend.	Wir **fuhren** letztes Wochenende auf die Farm.
Aber: We **didn't go** to the farm last weekend.	Wir **fuhren** letztes Wochenende **nicht** auf die Farm.

Ziel 4: Ich kann eine Detektivgeschichte verstehen.

○ **a)** Lies die Zeilen 1 bis 11 auf Seite 62 in deinem Buch und kreuze an, was richtig ist.

1. Was machen Luke und Sherlock im Park?
   a) Sie trinken Kaffee. ☐
   b) Sie spielen mit einem Fußball. ☐
2. Wohin gehen sie nach zwei Stunden im Park?
   a) Sie gehen ins Park Café. ☐
   b) Sie gehen nach Hause. ☐
3. Wen sehen sie vor dem Café?
   a) Sie sehen Olivia, Dave und Holly. ☐
   b) Sie sehen Mrs Abrihim und einen Polizisten. ☐

○ **b)** Lies nun die Zeilen 12 bis 24 auf Seite 62. Beantworte die Fragen mit Ja oder Nein und schreibe, wo du die Antwort gefunden hast.

1. Steht etwas über Unordnung im Text? ________ Zeile ________
2. Fehlt Geld in der Kasse? ________ Zeile ________
3. Schließt Mrs Abrihim das Café ab? ________ Zeile ________

○ **c)** Lies den Text nun zu Ende. Setze die richtigen Namen in die Lücken ein.

1. ____________________ finds the first clue.
2. ____________________ falls from the ceiling.
3. ____________________ has a ladder.

○ Ziel 5: Ich kann Informationen über Schul-AGs weitergeben.

Du kannst die Bedeutung eines englischen Wortes oft erraten, weil es im Deutschen ein ähnliches Wort gibt.

Verbinde die Sätze, die die gleiche Information enthalten.

1. When do you have some free time?
2. You can be creative in an Art Club.
3. Get some exercise in a Sports Club!
4. You can make new friends.
5. Meet people with the same interests.

a) Du kannst neue Freunde kennenlernen.
b) Treibe Sport in einer Sport-AG!
c) Wann hast du Freizeit?
d) Lerne Leute mit denselben Interessen kennen.
e) Du kannst in einer Kunst-AG kreativ sein.

Unit 4
Let's celebrate!

A

March

Red Nose Day

To do:
Buy a red nose.

B

______

______

To do:
Buy sweets.

C

______

______

______

To do:
Make a great costume.

D

______

______

To do:
Make a scary costume.

E

______

______

______

To do:
Make a big fire.

F

______

______

To do:
Buy a big tree.

1 Write the name of the month and the special day.

70/1

2 Tick ✓ the right box.

70/1

	right	wrong
1. The Notting Hill Carnival is in August.	✓	☐
2. People dance at the Notting Hill Carnival.	☐	☐
3. People wear scary costumes at Halloween.	☐	☐
4. People get new clothes for Red Nose Day.	☐	☐
5. On Bonfire Night people make a fire.	☐	☐
6. Eid is on 12th June.	☐	☐

3 (YOUR TURN) What's your special day?

71/4

Draw a picture of your special day in your exercise book. Write the name, when it is and what you can to do.

1 Complete the crossword.

72/2

Down ▼:
1. Olivia often … her friends to the cinema on her birthday.
2. Olivia has a great … for Jay.
3. Luke has chocolate … on his birthday.
5. Jay has a fancy dress … .

Across ▶:
4. Sherlock gives Luke a birthday … .
6. Olivia's costume is a big … .

2 (LISTENING) Listen and tick ✓ the right dates.

18
73/4a)

JANUARY 30	MARCH 6	APRIL 1	JULY 23	SEPTEMBER 12	NOVEMBER 19
☐	☐	☐	☐	☐	☐

3 Match the birthday activities.

73/4b)

picnic in the park | sleepover | theme park | fast food restaurant

1 

____

2 

____

3 

____

4 

____

74/8

4 Write the words.

a) Put the words in the right place.

often | never ✓ | always | sometimes

– | + | ++ | +++

never ______ ______ ______

b) Write about Sarah's Brithday. Find the right words from a).

I ______ eat cake on my birthday. I ______ have a barbecue – my birthday is in December! I ______ invite my friends to a party.

c) Write about Sam's birthday.

I ______ go to a theme park on my birthday. I ______ have a party at home, but I ______ get cool presents!

5 (YOUR TURN) Write about your birthday activities.

74/9

1. +++ I always have a chocolate cake on my birthday.
2. – ______
3. + ______

74/9

6 (WRITING) Write about their weeks.

a) Put the words in the right order.

1. Mondays • on • sometimes • my bike • ride • I

   I sometimes ride my bike on Mondays.

2. I • Tuesdays • go • to the park • never • on

3. I • have • Wednesdays • on • music lesson • always • a

4. on • watch • I • sometimes • with Holly • Saturdays • TV

5. often • make • I • Sundays • a cake • on

b) Write sentences about Sid's week.

1 

2 

3 

4 

1 (SOUNDS) [ə] and [ən]

164/G5

a) Which word is wrong? Cross it out.

1. costume • party • animal
2. barbecue • fancy dress party • English class
3. cool present • activity • easy game
4. elephant • fish • star
5. invitation • uniform • interesting book
6. week • day • hour

Erinnerst du dich?
a cake – an animal
Es kommt darauf an, wie das Wort ausgesprochen wird, nicht wie es geschrieben wird. Vergleiche:
an uncle – a uniform
a house – an hour

19 b) Listen, check and say.

2 (SPEAKING) Make a dialogue.

164/G5

a) Complete the dialogue with a or an.

Partner A	Partner B
I have ______ invitation to Emma's party.	
	Do you have ____ cool present for her?
Yes, it's ____ nice T-shirt.	
	Is it ____ fancy dress party?
Yes, it is! Let's all wear ____ funny costume.	
	You can be ______ animal – a cat or ______ elephant.
No, I want to be ____ famous star or singer.	
	Oh, OK. When is your birthday?
It's on 2nd July. Please come to my party!	
	Er – is it ____ fancy dress party?
No, it's ____ barbecue in the garden.	
	Great! I love barbecues, but I don't like costumes!

b) Act the dialogue with a partner.

1 Boxes, bags and bottles.

77/5

a) Match.

1. A box of
2. A bag of
3. A bar of
4. A bottle of
5. A packet of

20 b) Listen and write the price.

2 (SPEAKING) Ask your partner how much it is and write the answers.

77/5

Partner A: How much is the chocolate?
Partner B: The chocolate is £ 1.69

3 (SOUNDS) [tʃ] and [dʒ]

21
77/7

a) Listen to the words and write them in the right place.

			[tʃ]	[dʒ]
1.	cheese	cage	1. cheese	cage
2.	orange	chewing gum	2.	
3.	March	January	3.	
4.	jeans	chair	4.	

22 b) Listen and say.

In January I wear orange jeans.
In March I eat chocolate and cheese.

4 What's in your shop?

Wähle fünf von den sieben Nahrungsmitteln aus.

78/9

a) Draw five things on the shelves in the shop.

fish | chocolate | crisps | milk | oranges ✓ | butter | eggs

b) What's in your partner's shop? Write questions. Use "Do…?"

1. Do you have oranges?
2. ______
3. ______
4. ______
5. ______

c) Ask your partner the questions from b). He / She answers them.

5 Ask your partner about the things in his / her shop in exercise 4.

78/10

Where … ? | How much … ?

1. How much are the oranges? — They're 99p.
2. Where ______ — ______
3. ______ — ______
4. ______ — ______
5. ______ — ______

6 (WRITING) Write questions and answers about Ben's family.

79/11

1. Does he like Science?

   No, he doesn't.

2. ______________________

   ____

3. ______________________

   ____

4. ______________________

   ____

5. ______________________

   ____

7 Put the shopping dialogue in the right order.

79/12

- [ ] Thanks. How much is it for two sandwiches and one coke?
- [ ] Yes, here are the sandwiches.
- [ ] That's £5.70, please.
- [1] Hello. How can I help you?
- [ ] How much are they?
- [ ] Yes, do you have coke?
- [ ] Thanks. Here's your change. Have a nice picnic!
- [ ] Hi. I need some things for a picnic. Do you have cheese sandwiches?
- [ ] Yes, here's the coke. It's £1.50.
- [ ] They are £2.10. Anything else?
- [ ] Here you are. Thank you.

1 (READING) Match the pictures with the name of the costume.

80/1

- witch
- Superman
- carnival dancer
- pirate
- alien
- smurf

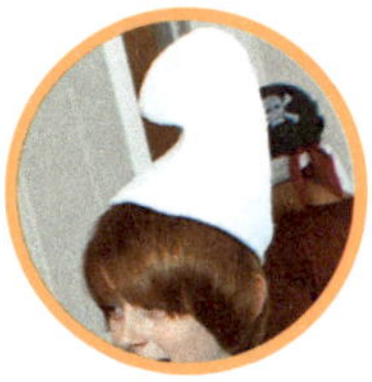

2 (READING) Read pages 80 and 81 in your book and choose the right answer.

80/2

1. Who invites his friends to the party?	a) Dave	b) Jay	c) Olivia
2. Who thinks Olivia is the pirate?	a) Jay	b) Luke	c) Holly
3. Who says, "I'm blue"?	a) Luke	b) Dave	c) Holly
4. Who wants to take a photo?	a) Jay	b) Jay's mum	c) Jay's dad
5. Who is late?	a) Olivia	b) Holly	c) the pirate
6. Who talks to the pirate?	a) Dave	b) Luke	c) Holly

3 Holly and the pirate

81/3

a) What do Holly and the pirate say in the garden?

costume | party | brother | friend | birthday | Who . . . ?

Holly: Who are you?

Pirate: ______________________

Holly: ______________________

Pirate: ______________________

b) Act the dialogue with a partner.

Frage deinen Lehrer / deine Lehrerin, ob du Verkleidungssachen mitbringen darfst.

1 (VIEWING) Who is it?

83/2

2 (VIEWING) Tick ✓ the correct box.

83/2

	right	wrong
1. Nathan wants to see his friends.	☐	☐
2. Laura is happy that Alicia is at the sleepover.	☐	☐
3. Laura asks Emily, "Why is Alice not here?"	☐	☐
4. Alicia has green pyjamas. *(Schlafanzug)*	☐	☐
5. Emily doesn't have pyjamas.	☐	☐
6. Nathan's friend Jack is at the sleepover too.	☐	☐

3 (WRITING) Make an invitation for your sleepover.

83/3

Ziel 1: Ich kann über Feste sprechen.

→ ◎ mi5sw9

What can you say about these special days?

Red Nose Day	November	wear … collect …
Halloween	March	wear …
Bonfire night	October	make

1. Halloween is ______. People ______.
2. Bonfire night is ______. People ______.
3. Red Nose Day is ______. ______ and ______.

7P
→ p. 62/1

Ziel 2: Ich kann über Geburtstage sprechen.

→ ◎ 8vh3gz

What does Jeff say about his birthday?

My birthday is on 15th February.

I ______

My ______

______

______

Jeff

15th February
(+++) get – nice presents
(++) – sisters – make – birthday cake
(+++) invite – friends – party

3P
→ p. 62/2

Ziel 3: Ich kann ein Einkaufsgespräch führen.

→ ◎ yc8g4v → ◎ 6ei838

You are in Mr Safi's shop. Finish the sentences.

1. Mr Safi: Hello. How can I help you?
2. You: Can I have ______ a bag of crisps, please?
3. Mr Safi: Here you are. Anything else?
4. You: Yes. ______ lemonade.
5. Mr Safi: Here you are. Anything else?
6. You: No, ______?
7. Mr Safi: That's £2.58, please.
8. You: ______.
9. Mr Safi: Here's your change.
10. You: ______.

4P
→ p. 62/3

Ziel 4: Ich kann einen dramatischen Text verstehen.

→ ⦾ cx3p3a

In Mr Safi's shop

Narrator: Jay is in the corner shop.
Jay: Hello Mr Safi. Can I have a box of eggs, a bag of sugar and a bag of sweets, please? I want to make a cake.
Mr Safi: Wow! You can make a cake! But with sweets in it?
Jay: No, they're for me!
Mr Safi: Here you are.
Jay: Thank you. How much is it?
Mr Safi: That's £3.89, please.
Jay: Oh no! The money! It's at home! Sorry, I must go –
Mr Safi: That's OK, Jay. It's your birthday present!
Jay: Wow, Mr Safi! That's nice. Thank you! You can come to my party too.
Mr Safi: Thank you, Jay, but I'm in the shop this afternoon.
Jay: OK. Bye!

Read the text. Then tick ✓ the correct box.

	right	wrong
1. Jay wants to put sweets in the cake.	☐	☐
2. Jay finds the sugar in the shop.	☐	☐
3. Jay's money is at home.	☐	☐
4. Mr Safi goes to Jay's party.	☐	☐

4P
→p. 63/4

Ziel 5: Ich kann Informationen über ein Stadtfest weitergeben.

INTERNET

The Old Town Festival takes place every year one weekend in August. There are exciting shows and activities for everyone.
Teenagers love the rock bands in the park. You don't need money. – The concerts are free!
Lots of people go to the Old Town Festival for a snack at one of the street stalls. You can buy Indian or Chinese food.

Beantworte die Fragen deines kleinen Bruders zum Old Town Festival.

1. Wann findet das Festival statt? ______________________
2. Muss man für alle Attraktionen bezahlen? ______________________
____
3. Was kann man essen? ______________________
____

3P
→p. 63/5

Lösungen online
p84t65

Ziel 1: Ich kann über Feste sprechen.

Einige Wörter und Ausdrücke bleiben übrig!

○ **a)** Schaue dir die Wörter an. Nimm zwei verschiedenfarbige Stifte und umkreise die Wörter und Ausdrücke, die zu „Halloween“ und zu „Eid“ passen.

special day for Muslims | wear a scary costume | “Trick or treat!” | November

collect money for other people | October | a big fire | on a different day every year

○ **b)** Schreibe über „Halloween“ und „Eid“ jeweils zwei Sätze.

Halloween is in ______________. People ______________________________ and say, ________________________

Eid is a ______________________________________. It is ____.

Ziel 2: Ich kann über Geburtstage sprechen.

○ **a)** Welche Wörter und Bilder gehören zusammen? Verbinde sie.

- get a p...
- have a p...
- eat c...
- wear a c...
- go to the c...

○ **b)** Schreibe drei Sätze über deinen Geburtstag.

1. I always ________________.
2. I often ____________________.
3. I never ____________________.

○ ## Ziel 3: Ich kann ein Einkaufsgespräch führen.

Setze ein Häkchen hinter die richtige Antwort. Was sagst du zum Verkäufer, …

1. … wenn du eine Flasche Milch möchtest?
   a) What is milk? ☐
   b) I need a bottle of milk. ☐
   c) Is the milk 85p? ☐
2. … wenn du wissen willst, was die Orangen kosten?
   a) How much are the oranges? ☐
   b) No oranges, thanks. ☐
   c) Can I have two oranges? ☐
3. … wenn du wissen willst, ob man Luftballons kaufen kann?
   a) Where are the balloons? ☐
   b) Do you have balloons? ☐
   c) Are the balloons very big? ☐

Ziel 4: Ich kann einen dramatischen Text verstehen.

○ **a)** Lies dir den Text auf den Seiten 80 bis 81 in deinem Buch noch einmal durch.
Wo stehen diese Informationen?

1. Holly ist eine Hexe. Zeile 5
2. Dave ist Superman. Zeile ___
3. Luke ist ein Schlumpf. Zeilen ______
4. Jays Mutter will ein Foto machen. Zeile ___
5. Olivia kommt später. Zeilen ______
6. Olivia ist eine Tänzerin. Zeile ___

○ **b)** Finde die richtige Antwort heraus. Setze ein Häkchen.

1. Warum reagiert der Pirat nicht, wenn die Freunde Olivia rufen? (Zeile 16)
   a) Olivia hört schlecht. ☐
   b) Sie will nicht auf dem Foto sein. ☐
   c) Der Pirat ist nicht Olivia. ☐

2. Wer ist der Pirat? Was meinst du?
   a) Amber, weil sie gerne mit Jüngeren spielt. ☐
   b) Shahid, weil es auch sein Haus und Garten ist. ☐
   c) Jamie, weil Jay ihn zur Party eingeladen hat. ☐

Ziel 5: Ich kann Informationen über ein Stadtfest weitergeben.

○ **a)** Mache ein Poster für das Woodside Festival. Finde die passenden Informationen und schreibe sie an die richtigen Stellen.

burgers | free | park | sports | salads | 3 days in July ✓ | pizza | Friday to Sunday | show

WOODSIDE FESTIVAL

When: 3 days in July,

Where: ______

How much: ______

Activities: ______

Food: ______

○ **b)** Vervollständige nun die Informationen zum Woodside Festival auf Deutsch.

1. Das Festival findet an drei ______
2. Es findet ______
3. Es kostet ______
4. Man kann ______
5. Zu essen gibt es ______

89/1

1 Read Tom's e-mail to his new friend in Australia.

E-MAIL

Hi Simon!

I'm your new friend in England. My name's Tom Williams and I'm 12 years old. I live in Manchester, a big town in the north of England. Here are some photos of me and my family: My mum and dad (Jayne and Dennis), my brother Sam (he's 16) and my sister Rachel (she's 10).

We live in an old house in Stockport Road and we have a garden. My best friend in our family is my dog Berti. (You can see him in the photos.) My sister has two guinea pigs. I like them, but I love dogs! Do you have pets?

I like football and I often play computer games. But my favourite free-time activity is music.

School is OK. I don't like History and French, but I love DT and music (of course!) and I have nice friends in my tutor group. My best friends are Adam and Karim. Do you eat lunch at school? We have a cafeteria and the food is good. The best lunch is pizza. My favourite food is chocolate cake. But we never get that at school!

Please write soon. Tell me about your family, your friends, your free time …

And please send photos!

Bye!

Tom

89/1

2 Complete the form.

Tom wants a new friend in India. Complete this form for him.

- Bevor du anfängst zu schreiben, musst du zuerst die E-Mail verstehen. Schau dir noch einmal die Tipps zu den Reading skills in deinem Buch auf Seite 35 an.
- Unterstreiche nun die gesuchte Information in der E-Mail und trage diese dann (möglichst knapp) in das Formular.

GLOBAL FRIENDS

NAME: ____________________

AGE: ____________________

ADDRESS: ____________________

____

PARENTS: ____________________

BROTHERS, SISTERS: ____________________

PETS: ____________________

BEST FRIENDS: ____________________

COOL SCHOOL SUBJECTS: ____________________

NOT SO COOL SCHOOL SUBJECTS: ____________________

SPORT: ____________________

FREE-TIME ACTIVITIES: ____________________

____

FAVOURITE FOOD: ____________________

89/1

3 Complete the form with information about you.

Brauchst du hier Wörter, die du nicht kennst? Schlage sie nach und merke sie dir. Du wirst sie in Zukunft brauchen, wenn du über dich selbst schreibst.

GLOBAL FRIENDS

NAME: ______________________

AGE: ______________________

ADDRESS: ______________________

____

PARENTS: ______________________

BROTHERS, SISTERS: ______________________

PETS: ______________________

BEST FRIENDS: ______________________

COOL SCHOOL SUBJECTS: ______________________

NOT SO COOL SCHOOL SUBJECTS: ______________________

SPORT: ______________________

FREE-TIME ACTIVITIES: ______________________

____

FAVOURITE FOOD: ______________________

89/1

4 Spell it right.

a) Copy this text.

Tom always celebrates his birthday with his friends. They listen to his favourite music. It's on a Wednesday this year.

Wie gut bist du im Abschreiben? (Von einem Text, nicht vom Tischnachbarn! ☺) Es ist wichtig, ganz genau zu schreiben – und das kann man üben.

____

____

____

____

____

b) Tausche Workbooks mit deiner Partnerin / deinem Partner. Überprüft gegenseitig eure Rechtschreibung auf der gesamten Seite.

Es ist oft schwierig, Fehler oder Ungenauigkeiten im eigenen Text zu finden. Jemand anderes kann das oft besser.

Unit 5
Where I live

1 Hi, I'm Jayden. I live in Manchester. That's a town__________ in England.

2 Our __________ is in that big house.

3 There are ______________ and there's a ____________ too. I love their ____________________!

4 In the summer I often meet my friends in the ____________ after school.

5 On Saturdays I sometimes go to the big ______________________________. My __________________ shop is the sports shop.

1 Put in the right words.

90/1

park | town ✓ | flat | shops | café | shopping centre | sandwiches | favourite

2 (LISTENING) Right or wrong? Tick ✓ the right box.

23
90/2

	right	wrong
1. Holly lives in Brook Lane with her mum and her sister.	☐	☐
2. She often goes shopping on Fridays.	☐	☐
3. She doesn't like swimming.	☐	☐
4. You can see London from a park in Greenwich.	☐	☐

3 (YOUR TURN) Make a poster about a / your town.

91/3

My favourite ... | There is ... | You can do / see ...

1 Put a circle around the odd one out.

92/2

1. evening	(day)	morning	afternoon
2. happy	tired	funny	guess
3. songs	trainers	T-shirt	jeans
4. pizza	flat	sandwich	chocolate
5. cinema	shopping centre	homework	swimming pool
6. went	did	bought	tells

2 (LISTENING) What are the right places?

24
3/4a)

Listen to the CD. Choose the right word.

1. (cinema) / sports shop
2. café / corner shop
3. swimming pool / sports shop
4. park / school
5. flat / shopping centre
6. swimming pool / house
7. park / cinema

In diesem Hörtext wird der Ort nicht genannt, du hörst nur Informationen darüber. Hör genau hin.

3 What can you do in these places?

3/4a)

1. garden: *Here you can* ______________________
2. shop: ______________________
3. playground: ______________________

4 Write the right word on the line.

3/4b)

1. On Friday we went to the *library* ________. The books there were exciting! — river / (library)
2. On Saturday my dad went to the ____________ and bought lots of fruit. — market / cinema
3. Then we went to the ______________________ and bought a present for my aunt. — department store / station
4. After that we walked in the park and saw fish in the ____________ . — supermarket / river
5. In the evening I saw some cool pictures in the ____________ . — museum / playground
6. I really like my ____________ . There are so many interesting places! — shop / town

94/9

5 Finish the sentences with the right simple past form.

watch | go | clean ✓ | play

1. On Saturday morning Olivia *cleaned her bike.*
2. On Saturday afternoon ______________________
3. In the evening ______________________ a movie.
4. On Sunday afternoon ______________________

95/10

6 Put in the right verb forms.

infinitive	simple past	infinitive	simple past
1. *have*	had	6. do	
2. play		7.	won
3.	went	8. open	
4.	saw	9.	bought
5. help		10. want	

95/10b)

7 Read what Jay tells his friend on the phone.

Put the activities in the right order. Use then or after that.

> Yesterday I went to the shopping centre at 11 o'clock. Oh no, I'm sorry. – First I had a sandwich in the café. That was at 10 o'clock. In the shopping centre I bought a birthday present for Dad. Then it was lunchtime. In the evening I watched a movie at the cinema. Oh yes, in the afternoon I did my homework.

First Jay had ______________________. Then he ______________________

● 8 Put in the right simple past form of the verb.

5/10b)

see | go | do ✓ | watch | buy | have | play

1. Sherlock did ______ lots of things on Saturday.
2. He ______ breakfast with Luke at ten o'clock.
3. Then he ______ a black cat in the garden.
4. Luke ______ a new football for him.
5. Sherlock and Luke ______ to the park and ______ with the football.
6. Then Sherlock ______ other dogs in the park.

◒ 9 (WRITING) Look at Dave's list and write down what he did.

95/11

TO DO

Do my homework!! ✓
Help Grandma in the kitchen ✓
Go swimming with Luke ✓
Buy a new computer game ✓
Make pizza for my family ✓
Phone Jay ✓

1. He did his homework.
2. He ______
3. ______
4. ______
5. ______
6. ______

❀ 10 (YOUR TURN) Act your weekend.

95/11

a) Stelle deiner Partnerin / deinem Partner pantomimisch dar, was du am Wochenende gemacht hast. Wechselt euch ab.

Example:
Lena: *(macht z. B. Schwimm-Bewegungen)*
Lukas: You went swimming.
Lena: Yes, that's right. / No, that's wrong.

b) Denke zurück an die Tiere aus Unit 3. Sage, welches Tier du bist und stelle deiner Partnerin / deinem Partner pantomimisch dar, was das Tier am Wochenende gemacht hast. Wechselt euch ab.

Example:
Lena: I'm Edgar, the elephant. *(macht z. B. Fußball-Bewegungen)*
Lukas: Edgar played football.
Lena: Yes, that's right. / No, that's wrong.

1 (SOUNDS) [aʊ] and [əʊ]

25
95/11

a) Which sound is it? Tick ✓ the right box.

	[aʊ]	[əʊ]
1.	☐	☐
2.	☐	☐
3.	☐	☐
4.	☐	☐
5.	☐	☐
6.	☐	☐

26

b) Listen and circle the [aʊ] sounds in blue and the [əʊ] sounds in red.

1. Don't talk about the weekend now.
2. Luke had a coke in town.
3. Let's phone Jay and say hello.
4. I don't like that brown house.

2 (SPEAKING) Where are the places?

95/11

a) One of you is A, the other is B. A puts these places on the map: A tells B where the places are.

swimming pool
school
Jenny's café

Example:
The swimming pool is in … Road / next to … .

b) B puts these places on the map:
B tells A where the places are.

museum
sports shop
cinema

Example:
The museum is in … Road / next to … .

1 Find the words.

96/1

a) Make four words.

Sun- | sat- | -day
sea- | -card | -side
post- | -nav

1. ____________ 3. ____________
2. ____________ 4. ____________

b) Cross out the wrong word.

1. You can buy …	2. You can go …	3. You can eat …
a postcard.	lost.	fish.
fish and chips.	to bed.	crisps.
the seaside.	by train.	chips.
a satnav.	swimming.	trips.

2 Look at the pictures and write the words.

96/2

1. Holly and her dad went to Margate by ____________  .
2. They walked on the ____________  and played ____________  .
3. Then they went to a ____________ 

.
4. Holly's dad had fish. Holly had ____________  . She's a vegetarian.
5. After that Holly bought a ____________  .

3 (SPEAKING) A card game

7/5a)

a) Make five small cards. Draw a picture on each card:
a car, a train, a bus, a bike, a boy / girl on foot.

7/5a)

b) Take a card and look at the picture. Lena starts.

Lena: I went to school by bike.
Lukas: Lena went to school by bike. I went to the supermarket by bus.
Katrin: Lena went to school by bike. Lukas went to the supermarket by bus.
I went to the playground on foot.

7/5b)

c) Play the game again. Make more cards with these pictures:
a submarine, a tram, a helicopter, a plane, a boat, a motorbike, a skateboard, an underground train.

Lena: I went to the cinema by plane.
Lukas: Lena went to the cinema by plane and I went to the swimming pool by boat.
Katrin: …

4 (WRITING) Holly's weekend

98/7

a) Write five questions about the pictures. The words under the pictures can help.

Margate • go

in the sea • go swimming

frisbee • play

fish and chips • have

buy • postcards

1. Did Holly go to Margate? Yes, she did.
2. Did she ______
3. ______
4. ______
5. ______

b) Read about Holly's day in Margate in your book on page 96 again. Now make short answers for the questions from a).

5 (YOUR TURN) Questions and answers

98/8

a) Write questions for your partner about his / her weekend.

1. Did you see your friends?
2. Did ______
3. ______
4. ______
5. ______

see your friends? ✓
go to the cinema?
have fish and chips?
buy ...?
do ...?

b) Ask and answer the questions from a). Take turns.

6 Put in the right question words.

98/9

Dave asks Jay about his weekend. Put in What, Where, When or Who.

1. ______________ did you go at the weekend? – I went to the park.
2. ______________ did you see in the park? – I saw my friends.
3. ______________ did you play in the park? – We played football.
4. ______________ did you do your homework? – I did it on Sunday.

7 Complete Olivia's questions.

99/10

1. Where ______________ that T-shirt? – I bought it at the shopping centre.
2. When ______________ to the shopping centre? – I went there on Saturday morning.
3. Where ______________ on Saturday afternoon? – I went to town.
4. Who ______________ there? – I saw my uncle.

8 (MEDIATION) Help a German tourist in Margate.

99/12

Du bist in der Touristeninformation in Margate. Eine deutsche Touristin, die kein Englisch spricht, bittet dich um Hilfe. Vermittle zwischen ihr und dem Angestellten im Büro.

Touristin: Kannst du ihn bitte fragen, ob es hier einen schönen Strand gibt?

Du: ______________

Angestellter: Yes, there's one big beach here in Margate and some small beaches too.

Du: ______________

Touristin: Sag ihm vielen Dank für seine Hilfe.

Du: ______________

1 What's the right order?

101/4

Put the sentences in the right order. The diary in your book on pages 100 and 101 can help you.

There was a storm with big waves. ☐

Rodney was OK, but scared. ☐

Jim Preston started his job on the Cutty Sark. ☐

Jim and Bert had meat and potatoes. ☐

Jim put bags of wool on the Cutty Sark. ☐

Rodney, the first mate, was in the water. ☐

They saw a big shark. ☐

Jim was sick all day. ☐

2 Put the words in the right box.

101/4

friend · storm ✓ · man · meat · water · hungry · shark · potatoe

sea	food	people
storm		

3 (WRITING) Use the words on the left and write Jim's diary.

101/4

20th September 1885

today • not see • sharks • water — Today I didn't see sharks in the water.

go swimming — I went swimming.

waves • be • cool — ______

21st September 1885

help • Rodney • with • bags of wool — ______

Then • put • them • ship — ______

______

22nd September 1885

today • go • town — ______

be • a lot of • shops — ______

buy • new diary — ______

103/2

1 (VIEWING) Look at the pictures. Tick ✓ the right answer.

Jinsoo and Marley are …

1

2

3

4

1. a) at the cinema. ☐
   b) at the market. ☐
2. a) in the café. ☐
   b) at the market. ☐
3. a) at the post office. ☐
   b) in the book shop. ☐
4. a) at the phone shop. ☐
   b) at the post office. ☐

103/2

2 (VIEWING) Who says it?

1. I'm so busy today.
2. Meet me at the bus stop.
3. Can I have one bag of popcorn, please?
4. Two fifty is your change.
5. Eight pounds fifty.

103/3

3 (SPEAKING) Make shopping dialogues.

a) Complete the dialogue with these words.

here's your change | a bag of sweets | Three pounds sixty, please. | Yes, sure.

A: Can I have ______________________________, please?

B: ____________________. Here you are. ______________________________

A: Thanks. Here you are.

B: And ______________________________ – one pound forty. Bye!

b) Make new dialogues. You need these things.

a bag of chips / crisps | a bar of chocolate | a bottle of coke

Ziel 1: Ich kann meinen Wohnort vorstellen.

→ ⦾ 37ej63p

What does Anna say about her town?

I live in Stoke.

____

____

____

Anna

live: Stoke
flat: Victoria Road
swimming pool: next to cinema
favourite place: park

3P

→ p. 78/1

Ziel 2: Ich kann über mein Wochenende sprechen.

→ ⦾ c72h2c

What did Jay say about his weekend? Finish the sentences. Use the simple past.

go to Dave's house | listen to music | see Ray-B at the shopping centre | do my homework

1. On Saturday morning I ______________________________
2. Then I ______________________________
3. In the afternoon I ______________________________
4. In the evening I ______________________________

4P

→ p. 78/2

Ziel 3: Ich kann mich über einen Tagesausflug unterhalten.

→ ⦾ jz5mi6 → ⦾ d9c5dv

Write what Charlotte says about her trip to Southend.

go • Southend • train

buy • postcards • shop

go swimming • sea

have fish • chips • café

1. ______________________________
2. ______________________________
3. ______________________________
4. ______________________________

4P

→ p. 78/3

Ziel 4: Ich kann Auszüge aus einem Tagebuch verstehen.

→ ⦾ s7xq8r

a) Read the pages from Jessie's diary.

Saturday, 4th May

Yesterday I went to London by train. My big sister Gemma lives here. We went to a big book shop this morning. I bought an interesting book about London. After that we went to the Cutty Sark in Greenwich by bus. It's a very old and beautiful ship. In the evening we had fish and chips in a nice café. What a cool day!

Sunday, 5th May

My last day in London. Gemma and I had breakfast at ten o'clock. Then we went to town. We got lost on the Underground. It was scary. A man helped us. Gemma bought me a poster of London for my room. Now I'm home with my mum, my dad and my dog.

b) Right or wrong? Tick ✓ the correct box.

	right	wrong
1. Jessie went to London on Friday.	☐	☐
2. She bought a magazine	☐	☐
3. The Cutty Sark is an old bus.	☐	☐
4. They had breakfast at 10:00.	☐	☐
5. They helped a man in the Underground.	☐	☐
6. Jessie has a dog.	☐	☐

6P
p. 79/4

Ziel 5: Ich kann touristische Informationen über Greenwich weitergeben.

Help a German tourist in the Tourist Information Centre.

Frau: Kannst du bitte fragen, wann ich auf die Cutty Sark gehen kann?

Du: ______________________________

Mann: It's open every day from 10 to 5 o'clock.

Du: ______________________________

Frau: Wie kann ich von hier nach Greenwich fahren?

Du: How ______________________________, please?

Mann: There's the train, the Underground and there are a lot of buses too.

Du: Man kann ______________________________

____

4P
p. 79/5

Lösungen online
xa2z37

Ziel 1: Ich kann meinen Wohnort vorstellen.

○ **a)** Welche Wörter brauchst du, um über deinen Wohnort zu sprechen? Umkreise sie.

chips Maths playground homework swimming pool
diary cinema school trainers

○ **b)** Schreibe drei Sätze über eine Stadt / ein Dorf (es kann dein Wohnort sein). Benutze die umkreisten Wörter in a) und diese Phrasen.

There is / are … | My favourite place is … ✓ | … next to …

1. *My favourite place is* ______________________
2. ______________________
3. ______________________

○ Ziel 2: Ich kann über mein Wochenende sprechen.

Vervollständige den Bericht über dein Wochenende.

saw | walked | was | went ✓ | bought | played | had

After breakfast on Saturday I *went* ________ to the sports shop. I ________ new trainers there. In the afternoon I ________ to the park. I ________ my friend there. We ________ football together. On Sunday I ________ lunch at my friend's house. It ________ very nice.

○ Ziel 3: Ich kann mich über einen Tagesausflug unterhalten.

Trage diese Ausdrücke in die richtige Zeile ein.

my dad | last Sunday | on foot | went swimming | to the seaside ✓
by bus | to the zoo | in June | my tutor group | played games

1. Where did you go? *to the seaside* ______________________
2. When did you go? ______________________
3. Who was with you? ______________________
4. What did you do? ______________________
5. How did you go there? ______________________

Ziel 4: Ich kann Auszüge aus einem Tagebuch verstehen.

○ **a)** Schau dir die Geschichte auf Seite 100 und 101 in deinem Buch an.
Was findet Dave auf dem Dachboden? Setze einen Haken.

1. Ein Kinderbuch über die Cutty Sark. ☐
2. Das Tagebuch seines Ur-Urgroßvaters. ☐

○ **b)** Was passiert an welchem Tag? Ordne jedem Datum jeweils zwei Antworten zu.

2nd June 1885	Der erste Offizier wird aus dem Meer gerettet.
	Der Aufbruch nach Australien
6th June 1885	Das Essen schmeckt wieder.
	Die Ankunft in Australien
8th June 1885	Jim mag den ersten Offizier nicht.
	Jim hat einen Freund gefunden – Bert.
11th June 1885	Jims erster Arbeitstag
	Jim sieht einen Hai im Wasser.
12th September 1885	Sturm auf See
	Jim ist seekrank.

Du brauchst nicht alles, sondern nur die wichtigsten Informationen zu übersetzen.

○ Ziel 5: Ich kann touristische Informationen über Greenwich weitergeben.

Beantworte die Fragen eines Touristen über das Royal Observatory in Greenwich.

1. An welchen Tagen hat das Observatorium geöffnet?

   ____

2. Was kostet der Eintritt für mich und meinen Sohn Alex? Er ist 12.

   ____

3. Alex interessiert sich nicht so sehr für alte Uhren. Gibt es andere Attraktionen?

   ____

   ______________________________ über Planeten.

4. Kann man dort auch etwas essen? Wo?

   ____

Hier geht es um das Sprechen.

109/5

1 Partner A: Find the way.

Look at the map. (Your partner has the same map but different information on it.)

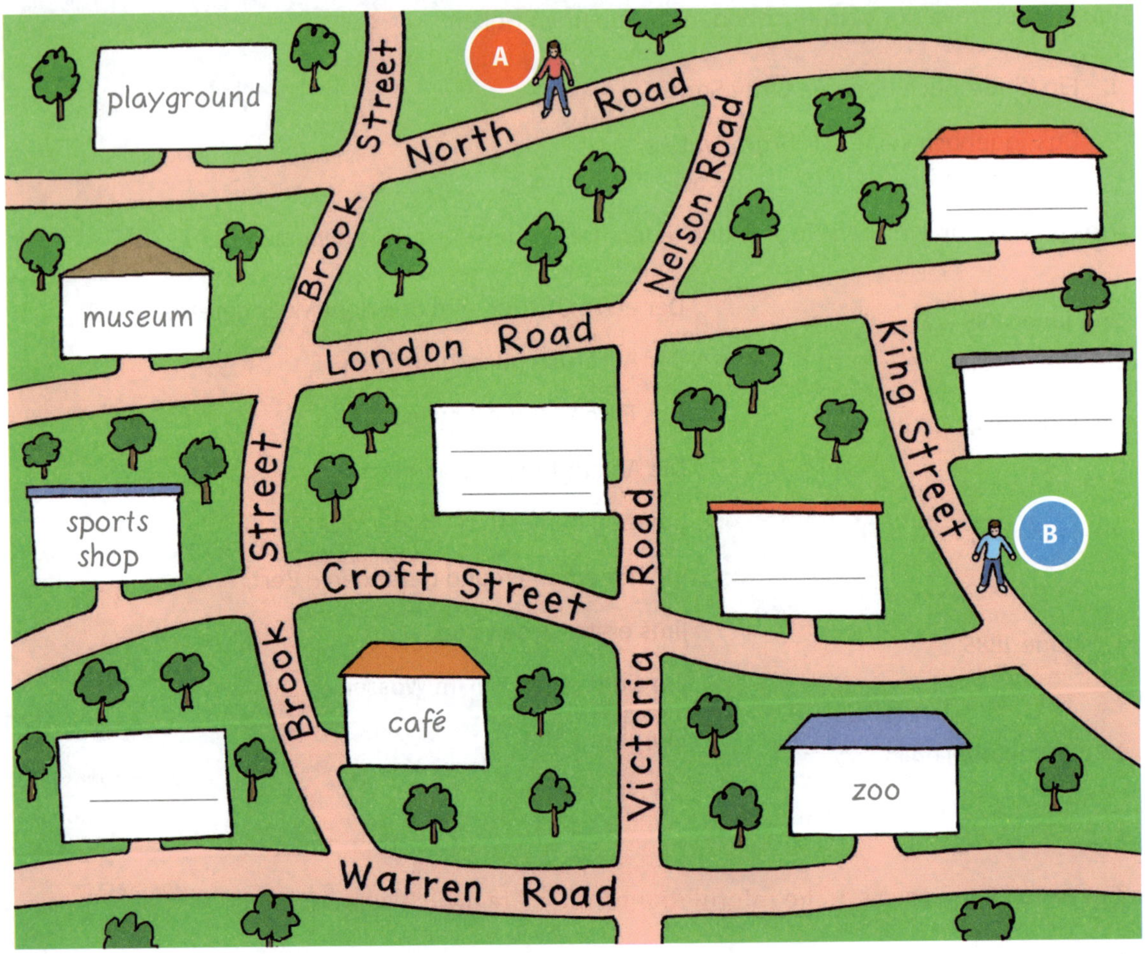

a) You are here, in North Road.
Ask your partner the way to these places:

cinema · park · hospital · station · shopping centre

Listen to your partner.
Go to the place and write the name on the map.

> Wenn du jemanden nach dem Weg fragen willst, benutze folgenden Satz: “Can you tell me the way to …?”
> Hast du etwas nicht verstanden?
> Dann frag nach:
> “Sorry, can you say that again?”

b) Now listen to your partner's questions and tell him / her the way.
He / She is in King Street.

> Wenn du jemandem den Weg erklären willst, benutze folgende Ausdrücke:
>
> - walk along …
> - walk straight on (until …)
> - turn left (into …)
> - turn right (into …)
> - next to
> - opposite

109/5

2 Partner B: Find the way.

Look at the map. (Your partner has the same map but different information on it.)

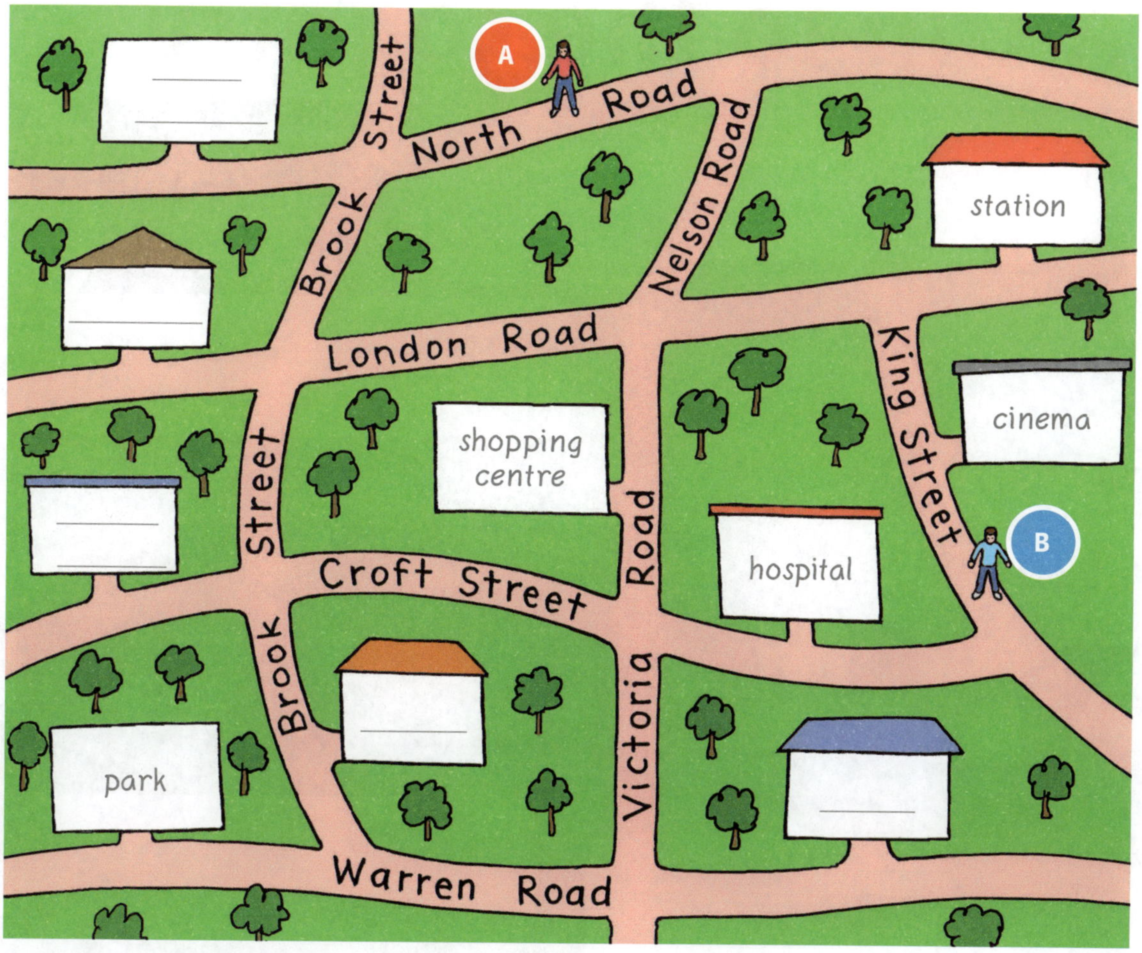

a) You are here, in King Street.
Ask your partner the way to these places:

zoo · museum · playground · café · sports shop

Listen to your partner.
Go to the place and write the name on the map.

Wenn du jemanden nach dem Weg fragen willst, benutze folgenden Satz: "Can you tell me the way to ...?"
Hast du etwas nicht verstanden?
Dann frag nach:
"Sorry, can you say that again?"

b) Now listen to your partner's questions and tell him / her the way.
He / She is in North Road.

Wenn du jemandem den Weg erklären willst, benutze folgende Ausdrücke:

- walk along ...
- walk straight on (until ...)
- turn left (into ...)
- turn right (into ...)
- next to
- opposite

Unit 6

A trip to the country

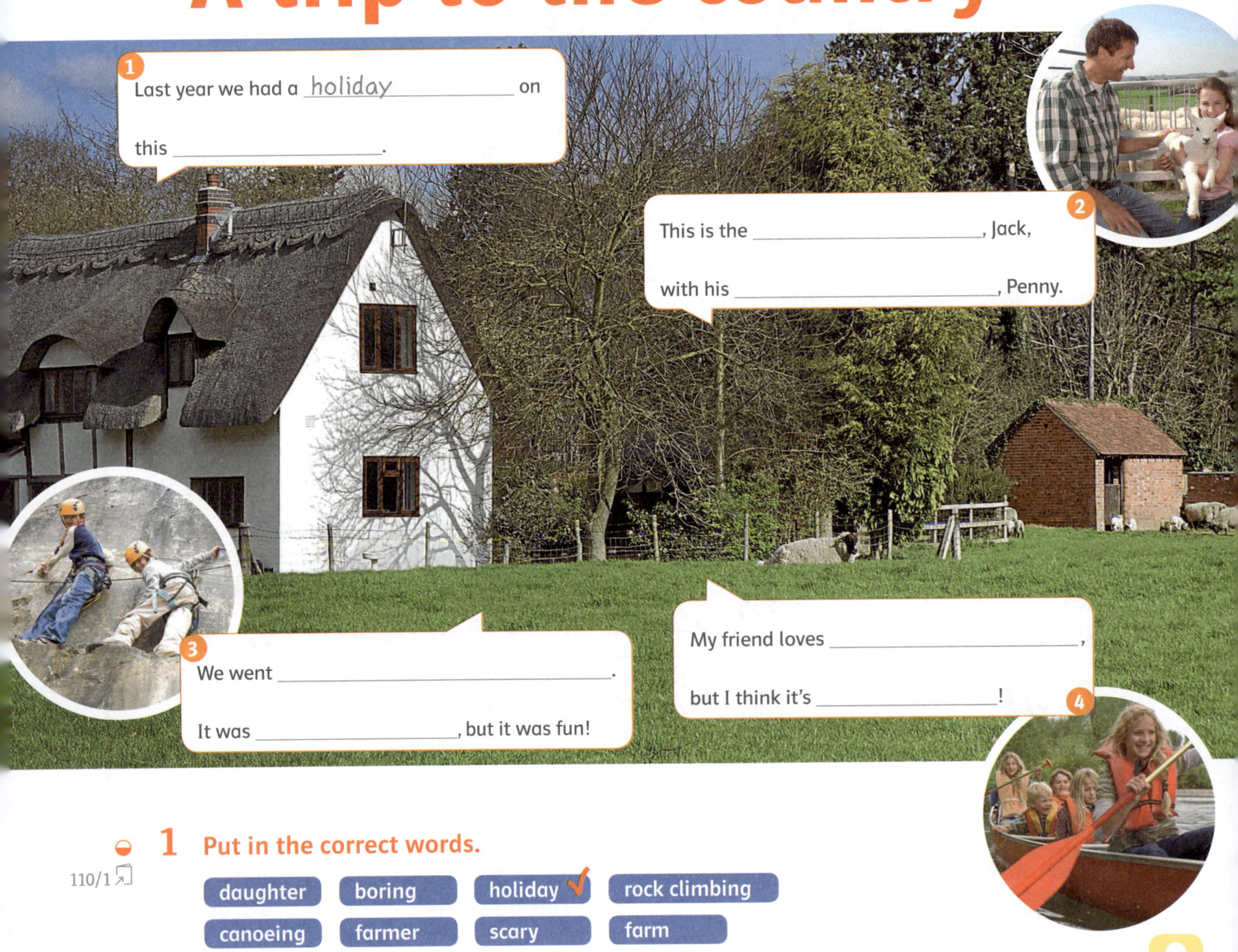

110/1 **1 Put in the correct words.**

daughter | boring | holiday ✓ | rock climbing
canoeing | farmer | scary | farm

111/3 **2 A poem**

a) Look at the pictures and finish the poem.

Come on, let's go, we're on our way!

A ______  is great for a nice day!

Sit on the ______ , sit on the ______ .

Play with the ______  – that's fun, of course!

b) Write your own poem in your exercise book.

1 Write the words for the clothes next to the numbers.

113/3

1. ______
2. ______
3. ______
4. ______
5. ______
6. ______
7. ______
8. ______
9. ______
10. ______

2 (SPEAKING) What do you need for a picnic?

13/4

a) You and your partners want to have a picnic. Say what you must take. Take turns.

Lena: We want to have a picnic and we must take a map.
Lukas: We want to have a picnic and we must take a map and apples.
Katrin: …

b) Now say what you needn't take. Take turns.

Lena: We want to have a picnic, but we needn't take a table with us.
Lukas: We want to have a picnic, but we needn't take a table or coats with us.
Katrin: …

3 Noun or adjective?

13/5

a) Put a circle around the right letter.

	noun	adjective
1. scarf	B	A
2. easy	S	O
3. nice	F	R

	noun	adjective
4. jeans	I	U
5. shoe	N	T
6. scary	D	G

b) Make an adjective with the letters in the circles. ______

4 Look at Dave's diary. Put in was or were.

114/8

Wednesday, 14th June

The night walk *was* ________ exciting and Mr Swindon ________ cool.

We ________ a big group. One boy ________ scared.

Luke and Jay ________ very nice to him. After the night walk

Holly said, "It ________ a great night!"

5 (WRITING) Write what Dave wrote to Olivia on his mobile.

114/8

class trip: exciting ✓	1. The *class trip was exciting.*
activities: interesting	2. ________
night walk: cool	3. ________
food: very nice	4. ________
rooms: great	5. ________

6 Complete Mr Swindon's text for the school magazine.

114/9

was (3 x) were (2 x) weren't wasn't

The Turners ________ very nice and friendly. And Barry ________ a very friendly dog, he ________ scary.

On the first day we went rock climbing.

That ________ exciting.

In the evening the students ________ very hungry! But they ________ tired. They talked until late at night. So I ________ tired the next day.

15/10

7 Questions for Mr Turner

a) What did the students ask Mr Turner? Put in Was or Were.

1. Were you busy today?
2. ______ Barry nice to the sheep today?
3. ______ the farm always for tutor groups?
4. ______ there other students from TTS here?
5. ______ your mum and dad farmers too?

b) What were Mr Turner's answers? Write the number of the question next to the answer.

Yes, I was. [1]
Yes, there were. [ ]
No, they weren't. [ ]
Yes, he was. [ ]
No, it wasn't. [ ]

15/10

8 Complete Holly's questions on the phone.

You need the right form of be and sometimes a question word.
Look at the answers for help.

1. Where were you yesterday? – I was at the cinema.
2. ______ with you at the cinema? – Dad was with me.
3. ______ the film good? – Yes, it was very good.
4. ______ the film about? – It was a science fiction film.
5. ______ you home late? – No, we were home at six o'clock.

5/11

9 A phone call

a) Find a partner. Put the sentences in the right order.

Hi! Is that you, *(Schülername)*? [1]
Hi *(Schülername)*! How are you? [ ]
OK. Great! [ ]
How was the movie? [ ]
See you soon! [ ]
I'm fine. I went to the cinema yesterday. [ ]
Bye, *(Schülername)*. [ ]
It was cool. Let's go to the cinema together next Sunday. [ ]

b) Act the dialogue with your partner.

27 115/11

1 (SOUNDS) [t], [d] and [ɪd]

How do you say the simple past form of the verbs?
Listen and put the verbs in the right place.

celebrated | helped ✓ | collected | wanted
invited | asked | cleaned | stopped

Wenn vor der ed-Endung ein 't' oder ein 'd' steht, spricht man die Endung [ɪd] aus.

[t] and [d]	[ɪd]
helped	________________
________________	________________
________________	________________
________________	________________

115/11

2 (SPEAKING) Make a dialogue.

a) Complete the dialogue.

stopped | invited | helped | watched
asked | collected | celebrated

Partner A	Partner B
Was your weekend nice or boring?	
	It was nice. I ________________ my birthday.
Oh, why wasn't I ________________?	
	Don't worry. I only ________________ my family. What did you do at the weekend?
On Saturday I ________________ money for Red Nose Day.	
	Cool! I ________________ last year. What about Sunday?
I went to the cinema. We ________________ a movie.	
	Was it good?
No, it ________________ after an hour.	
	Oh no. What did you do?
We went to a café.	

b) Act the dialogue with a partner.

1 (READING) What's wrong in these sentences?

116/1

Read the postcard on page 116 in your book. Underline the wrong word and correct it.

1. The night walk was boring. scary
2. They saw some birds. ____
3. They heard funny jokes. ____
4. Luke and Jay got lost. ____
5. They didn't wear their helmets. ____

2 What's the weather like today?

117/3

1. It's hot.
2. ____
3. ____

4. ____
5. ____
6. ____

3 Look at the weather in the pictures. What can't / can you do today?

117/4

have a picnic | go to a café | do sports | visit friends | go rock climbing | sit under a tree

1 

2 

3 

1. It's wet today. We can't have ____. Let's go ____
2. ____
3. ____

4 (SOUNDS) [w] and [v]

28
117/5

a) Listen and circle the [w] sounds. Then say the sentences.

Where were you at the weekend? – I went swimming with twenty penguins.

29

b) Listen and circle the [v] sounds. Then say the sentences.

Dave never invites Olivia to his favourite movies.

5 What didn't you do yesterday?

118/8

a) Write four sentences about what you didn't do yesterday.

- ~~go for a walk~~ ✓
- ~~see my friend~~
- ~~clean my room~~
- ~~eat pizza~~
- ~~go to school~~

I didn't go for a walk yesterday.

______

______

______

______

b) Make a double circle and tell your friends what you did yesterday.

6 (WRITING) Write four sentences about yesterday on the crazy farm.

119/9

ate / eat · fed / feed · said / say · slept / sleep · cleaned / clean ✓

1. The girl cleaned the pig, she didn't clean the horse.
2. ______
3. ______
4. ______
5. ______

119/9

7 What does Lucy ask Olivia about her friends' trip?

1. Did they feed the horses? – No, they didn't. They fed the chickens.
2. Did they go swimming? – No, they didn't. They went ____________
3. Did they see birds on the night walk? – No, they didn't. They ____________
4. Did they wear helmets on the night walk? – No, they didn't. ____________
5. Did they have a party? – No, they didn't. ____________
6. Did they eat pizza at the picnic? – No, they didn't. ____________

30
119/9

8 (LISTENING) What does Mrs Turner say about last year?

Tick ✓ the right answer.

1. The nice group was …
   a) from Wales. ☐
   b) from London. ☐
2. They went …
   a) canoeing. ☐
   b) rock climbing. ☐
3. The weather was …
   a) wet and windy. ☐
   b) hot and sunny. ☐
4. On a night walk a boy …
   a) got lost. ☐
   b) ate cake. ☐
5. They all went out with …
   a) candles. ☐
   b) torches. ☐
6. The Turners' dog …
   a) went on the tractor. ☐
   b) saw the boy. ☐

9/10

9 (YOUR TURN) Complete the postcard.

Use the words on the left or your own words.

boring, awful, brilliant, OK

windy, cloudy, sunny, wet

went for a walk, went canoeing, went horse riding, played cards

Hi ____________,

My holiday is ____________. On Monday

we ____________.

It was ____________! The weather was

____________ and ____________. Yesterday

we ____________.

See you soon.

____

1 (READING) Look at the pictures.

121/3

a) Read the story on pages 120 and 121 in your book again.
Find three mistakes in each picture.

b) Compare your mistakes with your partner. Did you find everything?

2 (READING) Match the sentences to the people.

121/3

1. He didn't answer his mobile.
2. They went to the river.
3. He went behind the sheep and pushed.
4. He fell in the mud.
5. She asked for help.
6. He saw the sheep.

3 What did Holly and Luke do?

121/4

a) Read about Rachel's problem.

It was breakfast time. Rachel was very busy in the kitchen, but there were no eggs.
Holly and Luke went into the kitchen.
"You're early!" Rachel said. "We need some eggs. Can you help me please? I'm so busy."
"Yes, of course we can help," they said. Rachel gave Holly and Luke a box.

b) Use the notes and write what Holly and Luke did.

went • chickens	1. *They went to the chickens.*
found • lots of eggs	2. ____________
put • box	3. ____________
gave • eggs • to Rachel	4. ____________
had • eggs • for breakfast	5. ____________

1 (VIEWING) Who has what? Write the right name under the picture.

123/2

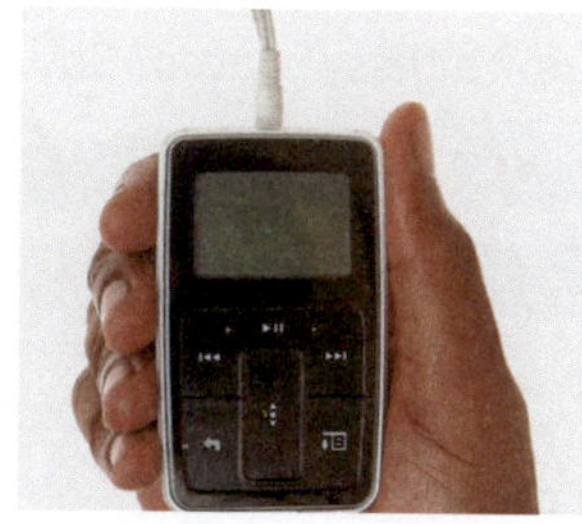

______ ______ ______ ______

2 (LISTENING) Look at the pictures ...

23/2

a) ... and **listen** to the film – don't watch it. Match the pictures with the sentences.

- See you here at four o'clock. ☐
- This smartphone tells me where we are. ☐
- Look here's the cache. ☐
- We must write our geo-names. ☐

b) Now watch the film and check your answers.

3 (WRITING) What do the three friends say?

23/2

Look at this picture from the film. Write a dialogue for the three friends and act the scene for your class.

______
______
______
______
______

Ziel 1: Ich kann sagen, ob mir ein Ausflugsziel gefällt.

→ ⊙ 5e9zz8

Would you like to go to these places? Say why or why not.

Greendale Farm ✓ | the river | animals ✓ | swimming | tractors | the water | interesting | cool | boring | cold

1. I would like to go to *Greendale Farm* because I think *animals* ________ and ________.
2. I wouldn't like to go to ________ because I think ________ and ________.

5P
→ p. 94/1

Ziel 2: Ich kann ein Telefongespräch führen.

→ ⊙ 4td44u → ⊙ n8x6n4

You are at Highfield Farm. Complete this phone call with your mum.

Hi ✓ | Bye | Hello | great | I'm fine | went horse riding

You: *Hi*, Mum. It's me.

Mum: ________. How are you?

You: ________. Guess what! I ________ yesterday.

It was ________. Oh sorry, I must go now. ________.

Mum: See you soon. Bye.

5P
→ p. 94/2

Ziel 3: Ich kann eine Postkarte schreiben.

→ ⊙ 942jr7 → ⊙ 863v8m

Look at the pictures and the notes. Write a postcard to your mum and dad.

Dear ✓ | exciting | See you soon | hot and sunny | went rock climbing | the farmer

Dear ________ Mum and Dad,

Hillside Farm is ________. On Monday

I ________. Yesterday I helped

________. It is ________

every day. ________.

____

5P
→ p. 94/3

Ziel 4: Ich kann eine Geschichte über eine Klassenfahrt verstehen.

→ ◎ px28fg

a) Read this story about three girls on a school trip.

Lily, Julia and Amy were at Northcote Farm. It was the last evening of their school trip. At 10 o'clock all the students went to bed. But Lily and Julia didn't sleep.
"Let's do something exciting!" said Julia. "What about a night walk?"
"We did that with Mrs Cole on Monday," said Lily.
"That was boring," said Julia. "No one got lost and it wasn't scary. Let's go on a night walk now, only you and me!" said Julia.
"Well, Mrs Cole says …" said Lily
"Don't tell me you're scared, Lily!" said Julia.
"Oh – OK," said Lily, "but don't make a noise!"
The two girls took some warm clothes, and three minutes later they were out of the house.
"It's cool out here in the dark!" Julia said. "No people, no noises, …"
Then they heard a noise, "Mooooo!"
"Listen, there are cows here! Can you hear them?" said Lily. "I don't like it! Let's go back!"
"Cows aren't scary," Julia said. "They're cute. Let's find them. Do you have a torch?"
But then a cow pushed Julia and she fell.
"Where are you Lily?" she called. "Help me! I'm here in the wet grass."
"Hm. So cows aren't always cute," Lily said. "Would you like to go back NOW?"

b) Right or wrong? Tick ✓ the right box.

	right	wrong
1. The three girls went on a school trip to a farm.	☐	☐
2. The students went on a night walk with Mrs Cole.	☐	☐
3. Julia, Lily and Amy went on a night walk.	☐	☐
4. Lily and Julia took their torches with them.	☐	☐
5. Lily says cows are cute.	☐	☐
6. Julia got wet because a cow pushed her.	☐	☐

6P
p. 95/4

Ziel 5: Ich kann Informationen von Schildern auf dem Land weitergeben.

You often see this sign in the country in England. Read it and answer the questions.

1. Wer darf diesen Weg benutzen?

 ____

2. Kann ich meinen Hund mitnehmen?

 ____

3. Was ist auf diesem Weg nicht erlaubt?

 ____

3P
p. 95/5

Lösungen online
qn5kr9

Du kannst Dinge (auch Ausflugsziele) mit Adjektiven beschreiben.

Ziel 1: Ich kann sagen, ob mir ein Ausflugsziel gefällt.

○ **a)** Schreibe die Adjektive, die etwas Schönes beschreiben, in die ☺-Spalte.
Schreibe die Adjektive, die etwas Unangenehmes beschreiben, in die ☹-Spalte.

☺	☹
interesting	

interesting ✓ · bad · brilliant · dirty · scary · cool · great · awful · exciting · boring · funny

○ **b)** Schreibe einen Satz über etwas Schönes und einen über etwas Unangenehmes.

☺ The ______________________ was ______________________.

☹ The ______________________ was ______________________.

○ Ziel 2: Ich kann ein Telefongespräch führen.

Was sagst du beim Telefonieren? Setze ein Häkchen in das richtige Kästchen.

1. Du nimmst das Gespräch an.
   a) It's me. ☐
   b) Hello. ☐
2. Du willst wissen, wie es dem anderen geht.
   a) I'm fine. ☐
   b) How are you? ☐
3. Du willst erzählen, dass es dir gut geht.
   a) I'm fine. ☐
   b) The trip is OK. ☐
4. Du verabschiedest dich am Telefon.
   a) Let's call a friend now. ☐
   b) See you soon. Bye! ☐

○ Ziel 3: Ich kann eine Postkarte schreiben.

Schreibe Lukes Postkarte an seinen Bruder Jamie. Wähle passende Wörter.

1. nice · cool · fantastic
2. fed the animals · went horse riding · had a picnic
3. go climbing · go canoeing · feed the chickens
4. hot · wet · cloudy · sunny
5. soon · on Saturday · next week

Dear Jamie,

It's ______________ (1.) here! Yesterday

we ______________________ (2.).

I didn't ______________ (3.). The weather

is ______________ (4.).

See you ______________ (5.).

Luke

Ziel 4: Ich kann eine Geschichte über eine Klassenfahrt verstehen.

○ **a)** Schau dir die Geschichte auf Seite 120 und 121 in deinem Buch an.
Wer kommt in der Geschichte vor? Setze Haken.

☐ ☐ ☐ ☐ ☐ ☐

○ **b)** Rachel hat drei Probleme. Welche? Setze drei Haken.

1. Sie weiß nicht, wo die Schafe sind. ☐
2. Ein Schaf ist in Gefahr. ☐
3. Sie kann ihren Vater nicht erreichen. ☐
4. Sie kann nicht zu den Schafen gehen. ☐
5. Die Klasse 7RS hat keine Zeit zu helfen. ☐

○ **c)** Warum wird Jay so schmutzig? Setze einen Haken.

1. Das Schaf rennt Jay um. ☐
2. Dave schubst Jay in den Schlamm. ☐
3. Jay schiebt das Schaf aus dem Schlamm und fällt selbst hin. ☐

○ ## Ziel 5: Ich kann Informationen von Schildern auf dem Land weitergeben.

Schau dir dieses Schild an. Beantworte diese Fragen auf Deutsch.

1. Was kann man auf der Hillside Farm tun? ______________________________

____

2. Wie lange kann man sich im Laden aufhalten? ______________________________
3. Was kostet der Eintritt für dich? ______________________________

CD zum Hörverstehen

Aufnahmeleitung: Ernst Klett Verlag
Redaktion: Joanne Popp
Sprecherinnen und Sprecher: Matt Addis, Anna Bentinck, Adriana Bertola, Brian Bowles, Jenny Brice, Elise Bugeja, Rosa Calcraft, DeNica Fairman, Jamie Goldberg, Paul Lincoln, Archie Lyndhurst, Jamie Murphy, Richard Pearce, Nigel Pilkington; Penny Rawlins, Elliot Reeve

Produktion: John Green, TEFL Audio, London
Tontechnik: Tim Woolf
Presswerk: Osswald GmbH & Co., Leinfelden-Echterdingen
Gesamtzeit: 28' 36"

Inhaltsverzeichnis der CD zum Hörverstehen
Hörverstehenstexte aus dem Workbook

Zusätzlich auf dieser CD:
- Alle Tracks des Workbooks als MP3-Dateien
- Alle Lesetexte des Schülerbuchs als MP3-Dateien